ENDURING FAITH

The Power of God's Great Love

Lorraine Parke

Enduring Faith

Copyright © 2018 by Lorraine Parke

All rights reserved. No part of this publication may be reproduced, distributed, or transmitted in any form or by any means, including photocopying, recording, or other electronic or mechanical methods, without the prior written permission of the author, except in the case of brief quotations embodied in critical reviews and certain other non-commercial uses permitted by copyright law.

Tellwell Talent
www.tellwell.ca

ISBN
978-0-2288-0132-0 (Paperback)
978-0-2288-0133-7 (eBook)

Acknowledgements

I would like to thank three people who have influenced me in writing a book about my life, God, my mom and Sarah Chaudherey. They, in their own way, encouraged me to share the blessing that has taken place throughout my life and made me aware of the power in sharing God's consistent grace in our lives. There were many people who played such a significant role in my life, and I consider them to be instruments used by God to show me His unfailing love. I could never forget their love and willingness to help me in the times of struggles, but the above three had a direct influence on the outcome of this book, and for that, I am truly grateful.

I thank God above all for writing my story (and the best is yet to come) and for giving me the tremendous strength needed to endure such hardship, with peace and patience. Thanks to my mom for being my backbone. When I felt weak and wanted to give up, she would sacrifice her own finances and livelihood to keep me afloat. She encouraged me the only way she knew how, and it was my mother's voice that I heard when I didn't know if or when I would complete my book. Lastly, Sarah encouraged me by writing a book of her own, while she was pregnant, mind you. She reminded me that people deserve to hear about the goodness of God played out in our life. Truly, without God and His guidance, I would be lost, dead even, but I thank Him for His love and dedication towards me.

What love, what mercies.

TABLE OF CONTENTS

Acknowledgements i

Preface v

Hope for a future 1

Spoken words and perception 7

Who is directing my li†wfe? 15

Love 25

Grace displayed in faith 31

Shelter in the storm 45

Enduring pain 63

Seeking peace 73

The fear of the Lord (what it really means) 87

Conclusion 95

Preface

My goal is to relate to you my experiences without harming the representation of people or places but to share with you Gods grace played out in my life.

I can never forget the love I have felt through God's grace pouring into my life. It is truly because of Him that I can write about His abundance of mercies in my life. I do not deserve any of it, but God has called me His righteousness through His Son's blood. Thus, He has seen me through the most difficult times of my life. As I write this book, I am reminded of my human limitations. I have realized that the accuracy of these reallife stories may not have taken place in the order written or that one or two details may not be as concise as I would want them to be. Due to the effects of my coma, I still have trouble recalling minute to minute details of particular stories told in this book. Nevertheless, this does not take away from all the blessings recorded. It has been these blessings that have helped me to endure my life trials with hope and encouraged me when I wanted to take my life. Yes, suicidal thoughts did go through my mind. God has been the only constant friend to me and has not abandoned me when people I trusted did. My hope is that through this book you will have a desire to encounter the Saviour as I have and, as such, I pray he will embrace and love you as He does to all those that love Him. If you are intrigued and want to experience the love I describe, then repeat after me:

> Lord, I am a sinner, and I apologize for my sinful ways, I need and receive your forgiveness of sin. I believe that You are the Only Begotten Son, Jesus Christ, and I receive you into my Heart today…Amen

The Bible, Romans 10:9 (King James Version) says, "That if thou shalt confess with thy mouth, the Lord Jesus, and shalt believe in thine heart that God hath raised him from the dead, thou shalt be saved."

If you said the prayer above, and you believe in your heart that Christ was raised from the dead, then welcome into the greatest family established here on Earth and in heaven. Find a bible teaching church, a church that desires to see you grow and become a disciple of the faith. Know today that you are loved and supported. Through this new journey, all victory belongs to you. Amen.

CHAPTER 1

Hope for a future

As far back as I can remember, God has been pouring out His favour upon me in deplorable situations and showing me His restoration power. Unfortunately, I did not always recognize His blessings and lived seventeen years without acknowledging His guidance or love.

To be honest with you I don't remember a lot about my life before the age of eight. I remember this age mainly because this was when my family and I moved to Woodbridge (a prominent Italian area), but also because this was the age where I slipped into a coma. That's right, yes…you read that right…I fell into a coma, no accidents, no traumatic event, nothing like that at all. I literally slipped into a coma. I have to reiterate this fact because people usually don't believe me when I tell them this for the first time, but it is true.

All I remember is that this incident took place after I came home from elementary school one day. I felt ill that day and my temperature began to fluctuate, feeling hot one moment and then cold another. This temperature change persisted for a while; my parents became concerned. As a result, my father took me to our family doctor, and it was in the doctors' office that I slipped into a coma. I remained in the coma for two weeks. This may not seem like much now because we now live in the land of technology but in the 1980s, this was a big deal. My parents, of course, were concerned and would visit me on a daily basis. Continually they would remind me (even now) that the doctors were convinced I had a 50/50 chance of living.

In the coma, I was told (by my parents) that I had to wear breathing tubes in my nose, an IV for feeding and had a tracheotomy performed on me during this episode because I had difficulty breathing. The scars left by the feeding tube and tracheotomy are still visible today. They are like my battle scars and remind me of God's grace and fervent love for me. After the tracheotomy was performed, the nurses had to remove thick, yellow mucus from my throat on a daily basis. Obviously, I don't remember a lot about the coma, but I do remember the day that I woke up…vaguely. I remember seeing snow falling which confused me a little since I did not recall it snowing before ending up in the hospital; nevertheless, I recall being in awe of the beauty set before me, in awe of the snow fall's beauty, it was as if I never saw such beauty before. My Aunt (my father sister) was also there, and I remember seeing both excitement and relief on her face. As a child, I didn't know if I realized that God delivered me from a near-death experience, but I was always enlightened to the fact that it was through the help of the Lord, as well as the prayers from the elders at the church I attended at that time, that gave me a second wind.

Like I mentioned before, I have always heard and appreciated the extent of prayers and concern of the elders in the church I was born in. Their support of my parents and me is something I will never forget.

However, overcoming the effects of the coma was not easy. As a result of the coma, I had to relearn how to walk again… in fact, I had to relearn everything again. I remember having tutors, trainers and specialists coming in and out of my home to rehabilitate me back to health, which included using the toilet, riding a bike, I had to relearn how to read and spell; I had to relearn how to use my small and large motor skills again…as if I were an infant.

I clearly remember having and using a silver walker, this was something I used on a daily basis with and without the help of the therapist as I relearned how to walk. Unfortunately, up to this day, I do not recall how many weeks, months or years it took to recuperate, but I thank God for helping me to regain the use of my bodily function and giving me the strength to overcome that aspect of my journey.

I vaguely recall the first time was able to go back to church, but, what I do remember clearly, is the last stanza of the first song I sang as my testimony when I was able to do so, the name of the song was "I'm coming up on the rough side of the mountain." and the last stanza of the song say, and I am doing my best to make it in. As I am writing this, tears are falling; the hope in God that I had then still rings true today, and I believe my journey is far from being completed, but I know with God as my anchor, he will help me rise above the storm.

Although I saw and visited many therapists I was left with a limp and continue to limp to this day, as well as, my right foot rotates outwards slightly. This deformity has caused me a lot of pain throughout my life and sometimes prevents me from being as mobile as I desired. Even as I write to you today, the limp and pain in my ankles remain the same, but I thank God for His blood that has redeemed me…In addition to this, after the coma, I also found myself back into the hospital on a yearly basis towards the end of the school year and for two weeks at a time. All the doctors who worked on my case were baffled for years with my condition and could not determine the causes for these episodes. Accordingly, they could never give my parents nor me an accurate answer or a clear depiction of why these episodes kept recurring.

After the coma, I remember being angry often. I was not sure if this was a result of the coma or if I was upset because of the bullying and negative treatment I endured from others, especially those I went to school with. After the coma, I quickly became a C and D grade student, and this fact occurred for the majority of my academic life. My teachers in elementary and high school all knew of my illnesses, and as result, many showed sympathy and, even worse, showed pity towards me. Accordingly, I was never really pushed or expected to excel further in my schooling. My assumptions today are that they (my teachers) either feared pressuring me or they simply gave up on me, period. I remember, vividly, my parents (although, wanting the best for me) saying one evening, "Do the best that you can, that's all we can ask." Along with this, some of my past teachers were convinced that I wouldn't go far educationally and were not shy to tell me this personally. Thus, school was a pastime activity. I mean, I thought about the future or I think I did…But in reality, I wanted to have a successful day and my hope was that one successful day would lead me to the next successful day and so forth. Above all, it was my Jamaican roots and Christian values that helped me become determined and created in me a passion for success, despite the many challenges I experienced in school.

Another negativity I endured while I was in school was racism. It was in the 1980s when my father moved us from Rexdale (a predominantly black neighbourhood) to Woodbridge (a predominantly Italian neighbourhood). In elementary school, my brother and I were the only two Jamaican-Canadian kids until grade four or five. I remember wet tissues were being spit towards me in class (I was never sure if the taunting was due to my colour or physical differences). From that time on (which is also the period I returned to school after the coma)….anger filled my heart, and I fought as a means of protection, or so I thought.

Punching, screaming, throwing kids into the closet or trash bin became a lifestyle for me, and I always got away with it because I was known as the poor girl who was in a coma and had no future. This internal anger grew within me, and I would internalize everything that was said and done to me. The racial attacks heighten when I went to highschool, along with my aggressiveness. I was that person that could not tolerate much and just the mention of my name from people I disliked or showed racism towards me angered me and made me lash out and become violent towards them.

I recall participating in many fights on the bus ride home during high school. It began in grade nine, and I remember having kids spit on my jacket, students hitting me on the head with a plastic object continually and chasing a boy down the street with a post because he attacked me on the bus…yes, an actual two by four post, only to have his mom call the cops on me with no charges being acquired!

Again, I found sympathy from my highschool teachers and the principal. This sympathy fuelled the rights I thought I had to protect myself from those around me. Before I knew it, I made friendships that also encouraged my violent behaviour, and, in fact, they would encourage me to fight for my rights and further still, they promised to fight for me when I felt I couldn't.

My family knew a lot about what I had endured, on two separate occasions, I remember vividly my brother and father sticking up for me in two separate attacks. In fact, my family encouraged me to stand up for myself…since they were not always there for me in times of need.

Although high school seemed to be a war zone for me on many occasions, I was still fortunate to make some longlasting friendships and as a result, I am the proud aunt of nieces today because of the friendships I made then.

I would never trade my experiences in for something else; these past experiences made me empathic towards others and gave me an awareness of internal emotional despair that people can experience regularly. Consequently, these experiences were the beginning of the many emotional turbulences that I would experience in the future.

CHAPTER 2

Spoken words and perception

I would like to start with a disclosure. I thank God for giving me the opportunity to be raised in a church like the one I was brought up in. There were many conflicts that occurred as a PK (Pastor's kid), but, in the end, my childhood church planted firm Christian roots in me. And taught me the art of total surrender towards my Lord and Saviour, and for that I am forever grateful.

Being a pastor's child was not easy and being a pastor's kid in a legalistic Pentecostal church was even harder. As a female, I had to endure more scrutiny, much more as compared to my brothers (I do not believe my brothers had the same experience growing up for the simple fact that they were boys and didn't have as much responsibility as I did). I remember being criticized for everything, petty things, like, my skirt was not long enough (it was knee length) or my hat was too small. The list went on and on…It got to the point where I would hear from friends that adults in our church were talking badly about me, and this would always break my heart! Relationships were and will always be something I cherish a great deal, so hearing people gossiping about me would always bring me to tears and make me cautious of those around me and their genuineness.

I was also a chubby girl for the majority of my life. Who am I kidding? I was fat. My parents would reassure me by saying the meds I had while hospitalized contributed my weight gain (since I was a normal-sized girl before the coma). For me, food became a coping mechanism. I loved it and it loved me. I would turn to food whenever I felt rejected or unloved. Because of my weight issues, and being raised in a Canadian-Jamaican culture, I remember being called many names like "fat" or told "boy, you're big" or "Ya big sah" (which is a Jamaican slang) pig, cow and more…I never felt recognized for who I truly was, and I always found myself in an emotional limbo. These names were inflicted on me in and out of church. In fact, I was rarely called by my real name.

Unfortunately, some of these names were also inflicted upon me at home. My parents, in the sociological world, would have been labelled as being authoritarian parents. My parents dictated what they expected from us (my brothers and me); they sometimes resorted to name calling to get their point across. We, in return, were not permitted to relay our feelings. If we did, we would be considered rude and would have even been spanked for any opinions stated that were not validated by our parents, mainly our father. And I was opinionated. So, you can imagine the many consequences I endured. This treatment could have very well contributed to my early aggression, my brothers were not exempt from the receiving end either, although they did not communicate as much as I did before and after our punishments. My brothers and I had many conflicts with each other, and I recall my brothers saying negative, hurtful thing to me or being physically abusive to me. It got to a point where I felt bombarded with negative talk.

Many times, I asked the Lord "Why am I here?" and "Why couldn't I have died in a coma?" and "Why do I feel so alone?" Even though I recall some rough patches in our home, I also remember events where we would take family trips to Wild Water Kingdom, Canada's wonderland and the like, but it was the *negative talk* that most influenced me. The conflicts in my head became larger than anything else, and I was not happy.

My brothers remind me, even now, that they remember finding me in my room with the lights off, crying. This happened more often than it should have. Although I was not happy with my life, I always knew God was with me, and knowing this is what kept me alive. Coincidently, what people saw when they encountered me was my smile without realizing that I was hurting inside.

At the age of nineteen, I remember going to church with my parents one Sunday morning. I would not categorize this service as a special service but something special happened to me. I remember the speaker that day was a pastor of one of the sister churches within the church where my father was the head overseer. That afternoon, she gave an altar call. As I stood before her, she placed her hand on my heart and said, "Despite the smile on your face, your heart is hurting, and God sees the hurt." I may be paraphrasing what was told to me that day, but the words brought tears to my eyes, and I felt God's love, concern and understanding. Amid my sorrow, God could empathize with my innermost hurt, which gave me the comfort and, ultimately, the resiliency I needed to continue for that day and weeks to come. This is one example of God's love that I experienced as a teenager. Two years prior,

I gave my heart to the Lord. It took place in my room, and it is one of those experiences I would never forget. That day, I had come home from the hospital. It was during one of the two-week episodes. My hospitalization happened during summer break. I remember entering my room feeling emotional…gratitude was one of the emotions I felt…I was grateful to Jesus. I collapsed on my knees. I recall telling Jesus how grateful I was and couldn't believe that He would spare my life again from sickness. I told Him that I realized I could have died, being older, and especially because I understood the difficulties I had endured regarding my liver during my stay in hospital.

Yet, I strongly felt like God kept me on Earth for a reason, a purpose. My liver complications could have harmed me, but He, Jesus, saved me once again. I told God that I wanted to give back to Him all that He has given me. That I wanted to surrender my life to Him, that I wanted to be used by Him.

Being raised in my Christian home, I was fluent in "Christianese" and used it within this particular prayer, but I don't think I was ready for what I had just declared. My initial transition was quite immediate. After that visit to the hospital and my experience with Christ's love, I remember returning to high school with a calmness, a more genuine smile and an internal peace. What I recall the most were the expressions on people's faces on the bus on the way to school and back. They seemed more nervous and unsure of what to expect from my joyous but (to them) very odd behaviour. I sat alone that day, and everyone who saw me seemed to be in disbelief, unwilling to risk approaching me.

I want to stop and testify to God's greatness. Because after this last episode of illness (which coincides with me accepting

Christ into my life), I have not been back in the hospital. After I gave my heart to Christ, He has spared me from further illness that could have resulted in more hospital stays.

I give God all the glory!

Nevertheless, life was still a constant battle, emotionally, and I never thought I was good enough or had anything worthwhile to give anyone. During this heartache, God was the one who showed me the most love and the consistency of love that I desired. But I always doubted if I was a good enough Christian because of some of the influences around me and because of some of the religious beliefs I grew up with.

If you were fortunate enough to have been raised in a Pentecostal church, then you know that the next step to take after becoming saved and being baptized is to be filled with the spirit, with the evidence of speaking in tongues. This did not happen for me right away, and the longer it took, the more I prayed. I remember feeling jealous when my friends in church were filled with the Holy Spirit, and I did not. This was a big deal for me. I wanted more of God, especially because He represented true, consistent love for me. So, I continued yearning and reading about His greatness, His love and mercy.

One Saturday evening, there was a conference at another church and the guest speaker was closely affiliated with our church at that time. Coincidentally, a bunch of the congregation from my father's church decided to go hear this preacher. With excitement in the air, we made a conscious effort to arrive at the conference on time (not Jamaican time) and sat close to one another. I do not recall the message I heard that day, but I do remember an altar call being summoned, and this altar call was geared toward receiving the Holy Spirit. Just what I needed...

especially since I was still not empowered by the Holy Spirit at the time of the conference…I went to the altar that evening with an expectation of the Holy Spirit pouring with love upon me. The minister shared with us at the altar that night about God's willingness to endow those at the altar with His power so that we could be strengthened to do God's work…God, I thought, you know that I need your strength…I can't do this on my own. I must have been at the altar for hours, and I was pleading to God…I need you! In the mist of my prayer to God, our family friend approached me.

He proceeded to lay his hands on me and began to pray with me. After his prayer, he impelled me to repeat after him…little did I know, but He was manipulating an experience in my life that was important to me, but I did as I was told. When I left the altar that night, I felt guilty, betrayed, and confused. *What happened? This could not be it*, I kept saying in my head. I remember as I was driving home from this abnormal event, I felt an urgency to talk to God about what had transpired. When I got home, I did exactly that. Since that day, I have yearned for an authentic relationship / experience with my Lord and Saviour. I was filled with His spirit and spoke in an unknown language but because of my previous experience, I struggled for years and wondered if the second encounter was from God or if it was something else.

The next spiritual awakening I experienced resulted in me lying on the floor, my eyes drenched in tears and me uttering the words "I am not worthy." This event happened at my father's church, and I am unsure if it was at a regular Sunday service or a special event, but despite my negative and self-inflicting prayer, a brother in Christ knelt beside me and reminded me that I was worthy of God's glory and His grace and favour. I will never forget that day. For me, it was another reminder that God wanted to dismiss all the fallacies I believed about myself, and an introduction to my spiritual journey with my living, but oh so loving, Saviour.

CHAPTER 3

Who is directing my life?

As far back as I can remember, it has always been important for me to work in an area that I loved or enjoyed doing. I have always loved helping others. As a matter of fact, I remember bandaging my brothers' bruises with toilet paper whenever they fell and hurt themselves. Spontaneously, I remember using the sentences like "I love to love people," despite not feeling their love in return. I can remember congregates in my father's church and friends complimenting me on my kindness and stating things like, "You look like a nurse." Thinking this was a sign from God. I considered nursing as my career path. My parents knew that this career was a profitable one and would help me to secure a good future, so they encouraged me as well. As a result, I believed that this profession was my future, my destiny; I mean, how could it not be? I loved people, I loved helping people, plus if people thought I looked like a nurse…this was obviously my destiny.

I felt, too, as if I had the support to follow through in this career, if help was needed.

So, when applications for college were available, I went ahead and applied to four or five colleges with nursing programs. I was so excited at the prospect of college and beginning a new, healthier phase. Sure, I still had ideologies or thoughts of how I would accomplish this goal but, in the end, I was sure that God would see me through. I mean, if He brought me through sickness and close to death, He would surely see me through this. I am not sure how long I waited before I got replies back from the first few colleges, but I can still feel the heart beats in my chest as I read the first response to my college application:

> Thank you for your interest in the Nursing Program at _____College. We received many interesting and excellent applications, a few we were able to accept this year. We reviewed your application carefully and noted several strong features. There is rigorous competition for entry into our graduate programs, and your application was not among those that we were able to accept.

One by one, rejection after rejection, these letters came in. In my room I held my tears while rejecting the belief that I did not have a future in sight. Suddenly, a thought from my past crept in and said, "I told you that you could only make it so far." My tears felt like a rush of waves, and I couldn't hold back my tears any longer. I sobbed, and my mind became infiltrated with "I can't or "How can I…."

This was one of the most helpless times, and my heart turned to God in my distress. "How will I make it?" I asked God. In the middle of my hopelessness, God set my thoughts to music. I turned off the lights in my room and turned on my cassette player (this was the '90s) while lying helplessly on my bed, and the first song that I heard was "I know that I can make it" by Kirk Franklin.

After listening to this song, I felt hope rising in my soul. And God embraced me. Literally, He hugged me, and it was as real as it would be if a friend or family member hugged me. Again, tears came rushing, but this time, it was tears of joy and love that I felt for a Saviour I have not seen, but yet I had experienced Him consistently in the darkest times of my life.

After the disappointing letters, I got right back to the drawing board, did some research and became aware of a general arts and science program, a two-year program with entrance into the nursing program when all your courses are passed. I applied and got in. Two years later, I was in the nursing program and felt a sense of pride in my achievements and vigour for my academic accomplishment. My pride came from the success of attaining my goal and, secondly because I was in the nursing program, which was a dream I had established for myself.

It didn't take long before I doubted if nursing was for me. I always found myself in a place of barely passing my exams and courses. I became frustrated but was still determined to succeed in the courses because I wanted to believe the Lord was leading me, and he was.

In addition to the failure I was experiencing in school, I began noticing some signs of anxiety…I lived away from home (at this time, I stayed with family friends from my father's church; they lived in Scarborough, and their home was thirty minutes on public transit to my school). Whenever I left their home to go to school, I would visualize cars hitting me as I crossed the street or falling into traffic and being hit by an automobile. Initially, my remedy for my irrational visions was to shake my head right after as if they could fall out. Needless to say, this did not work. The verse in the Bible that declares, "And no weapon that forms against me shall prosper" became my anthem. Every time I visualized getting hurt (which happened every time I commuted), I would mutter this verse to myself. I also remember experiencing stomach pains and diarrhea in stressful situations like exams, tests, and when I worried about being late for school or any other appointments I had. These are secrets I've concealed throughout my life. I was too embarrassed to share them with anyone, and this included my family, friends and family doctor. Along with being embarrassed, I didn't want to give people another reason to judge me.

After completing my second year of nursing, I found myself more confused than anything else. I started a placement in a hospital but noticed that I would spend the majority of my time with patients, talking instead of completing the work that I was assigned by my shadow nurse. I also found the physical aspect of this job was overwhelmingly difficult for me to accomplish; this was due to my known limitations.

As a result, I wondered if it was for me. So much so, I took an additional year off, to work. Considering my next steps was not an easy chore because I deeply believed in doing what I was called to do, and I loved working with people. During the '90s, I wasn't sure of another course would complement my passions. So, after a year of working, I enrolled in the Personal Support

Worker Program, another area in the healthcare field but without the intensity of nursing, although, still physically demanding. After passing this course, my professors convinced me to enter into the Practical Nursing Course.

In the Practical Nursing Program, I was fortunate to meet some wonderful people who became my friends throughout the duration of my college years, but one person I met in the Register Practical Nursing Program changed my life forever.

This friend, I will call her Sue, was a recent Canadian immigrant. She came from Africa with the desire to create a better life for herself, while having the ambition to help her family back home. I remember some of our conversations. In one, she spoke about the pressure she felt living here, in Canada. Her stress derived from balancing work, school, and having the responsibility of providing financially for her family back home. She revealed that she was the main provider for her family, and they were not shy in reminding her of this. Along with disclosing her responsibility towards her family, she also confessed that their dependency made it difficult for her to live well on a day-to-day basis. I gave Sue my phone number and told her to call me anytime. I was not sure if I could help Sue, but I wanted her to know that someone was there to support her and would also be there for her if she needed someone to talk to.

One night, without expecting it, she called me, but something was unusual about her voice. Acknowledging the awkwardness in her voice, I asked Sue, "Are you okay?"

She replied, "It hurts," and said this phrase for what seemed to be an eternity, and I was scared.

"What hurts Sue?" I asked nervously.

"It's like a sharp pain."

"What are you talking about?" I breathed in deeply. She hung up. I looked at the phone and wondered, *what should I do now*? I was scared for Sue, the most concerned I have felt for anyone in this particular period. I could only cry. (When I was younger, my friends at church named me the town crier, because I cried in every situation, happy or sad.)

I wanted to help Sue in the best possible way because I knew I was the only person she had, locally. So, I did what I knew best...I prayed. I asked God for direction because I had nothing... no address, no phone number to reach her, nothing. After seeking God's direction, I called 911 and explained that I got a freighting call from a college friend. I told the operator that she made references of hurting herself and then she hung up before I could totally understand what she was saying. "I am afraid that she will hurt herself, and I don't have any contact information for her. I am not sure if you could trace the number of her call to find her, but I am scared, please help." In response, the operator assured me that they would do what is necessary to find my friend and told me not to panic...easier said than done.

I am not sure how many days later it was because it felt like months, but her professors alluded to me that she had been admitted to the hospital. After I was provided with facts about her hospital stay, I went to visit her and did so until she was discharged. I assisted her with handing in her assignments to her professors.

My desire was to be there for her and give her the support she needed. Her teachers complimented me on the friendship I showed towards Sue but also asked me if I was in the counselling program. "What's that?" I asked, but reply with a sharp "No," but my curiosity was illuminated.

With my parents' permission, I invited Sue to stay with me for a few weeks after her discharge from the hospital. I never wanted her to be alone and knew that this would be her destiny if I did not extend an invitation. I believed Sue knew this as well because she welcomed the idea and, indeed, stayed with me and my family until she felt like she could go back home. During her stay, Sue accompanied me and my family to church. I do not believe she was familiar with the church routine, but after a few visits, she appreciated the family experience gained in church and thanked us for our generosity and love shown.

After college, unfortunately, we did not stay in touch, but I was privileged enough to see her after my university studies. One day, I went to a mall in a different neighbourhood and saw her shopping. We spoke for a bit, and I learned that she was going to church with her husband and child; she also disclosed that she was in a better state of mind since the last time we saw each other. Hallelujah! This might seem like an interruption in my story, but I needed to point out how faithful God is when you surrender to his authority.

I was privileged to have God use me in Sue's life so that her life was renewed both physically but spiritually. The greatest gift I could have received was to know that Sue is now living an abundant life through Christ and that He restored her where she lacked hope. God is so good!

He also reassured me and my abilities as a counsellor as such, I took a real interest in the course Sue's teachers mentioned, the Human Service Counsellor Program. I sought help from a career counsellor, and I took a test to see if the course was compatible with me...and it was. I applied for the course and got in without a hitch, so I transferred to the Human Service Counselling Course without saying a word to anyone. When I did have the courage to tell my family that I transferred programs, they responded like I had made the worst decision ever, but the deed was done and a new chapter started whether I liked it or not. Once I was in the program, I noticed that my grades we're remarkably better. In fact, the C and D that I received in the nursing program turned to A and B in the counselling program. Things became clearer, and I had dreams and aspirations again for my future. I should also mention that my parents changed their tune regarding the program when they saw my marks.

Although many positive changes occurred once I switched courses, that didn't exempt me from having challenges.

I remember one incident during my college placement. I was working at an organization that will remain nameless (my goal is to relate to you my experiences without harming the representation of people or places), a mental health centre that offered programs, life skill groups, group therapy, cooking groups counselling services, case management and an Assertive Community Treatment Team (ACTT) program for clients attending this organization or who were registered.

My supervisor at this time was, ironically, named Lorraine. One day, I had the privilege to learn about their ACTT team: a team of doctors, nurses, social worker, counsellors, settlement workers and more. They would travel to different shelters throughout the day and give aid to the clients within them. I found this to be an amazing concept and wondered what it would be like to be part of such an inspiring team.

I spoke to my supervisor and shared my excitement and possible aspirations of one day being a part of such a team. She told me that this would never be a possibility for me because I needed a university degree. For me, she was implying that I would never be able to attain a university degree. Boy, did her comment upset me! Having a history full of naysayers didn't help.

I didn't want to remember nor harbour that sort of negativity. I wanted to believe that I was now experiencing a new chapter, I wanted to believe God's promises over my life, so I needed a technique that would help me deal with the anger I felt that day. I realized that I needed to remove myself from my supervisor, and I did. I went into the office that was assigned to me, and I journalled (something I learned throughout my counselling course) my feelings about what had happened. I was surprised to notice that I was journaling past incidences that contributed to my frustrations and disappointments. This tool helped me tremendously, so I began implementing the tools I was learning in my classes as ways to deal with all the negative voices in my head.

Taking the course was a rewarding time for me, considering my journey, and I looked forward to my graduation day. My mother and middle brother came to support me, but my father did not see the need to support me on graduation day since it was a college diploma and not a degree. His perception and attitude contributed to my feelings of worthlessness. I refused to let his actions cloud the accomplishment I felt.

Several months after graduation, I landed a job in a group home and began working with youths who had social issues and were state wards (this is when the court or state becomes their guardian). Like any job in the initial stages, it was rewarding. But after a few incidences with the youth and conflicts with legal organizations, the excitement began to dwindle.

Additionally, this job was in Brampton, but I lived in Woodbridge with my family. Commuting on public transportation took an hour, including returning home, which was not easy for me since my shifts were mainly night shifts, but if there were one thing that I have learned throughout my life was to never give up! Now, persistence and faith in Christ had become a key way for me to live!

My overnight shift at the group home was usually 11 p.m. to 7 a.m. I am sure you can imagine some of the strain I endured during these times. Usually, I was the only worker on this shift, even though I had help during this shift from 11 p.m. to 12 a.m. My coworker in the previous shift and I would ensure everyone did their bedtime routine. We documented and discussed the events of the previous shift and ensured that all the youth went to bed on time. For the remainder of my shift, I would be alone in this coed house.

On occasion there would be an uproar. I recall one episode where a male client came home past his curfew with a knife in his possession. I found the knife after I completed his bed check. Being alone on staff in this situation was frightening for me simply because the knife was a fixed blade hunting knife, my job was to control the situation by gaining access to the knife. This young male did not want to give me the knife and, instead, ran away from the home. After completing all the documents necessary and getting in touch with the local police and Children's Aid Society, I began deliberating my current role at the group home and the dangers that came with it. While I gained a lot of insight from that job, I also quickly noted that I was called for more.

CHAPTER 4

Love

This chapter is not like any other that I have written before, but I wanted to elaborate on my feelings or struggles that I encountered growing up, not just the physical limitation. One thing that I have learned through my schooling is that, as humans, we all have mental health issues. It is how we cope with them that determines whether they become mental health problems or remain as issues. It is the compound of surrounding issues that eventually affects one's ability to function successfully and not just survive.

I felt unloved and unwanted. My psychological abandonment started during the acknowledgement of my physical limitation and was confirmed through the constant negative comments I heard from those around me as well—rejection from those I respected and loved the most. The rejection limited the positive thoughts I had about myself and, in retrospect, it contributed to the struggles I encountered as I strove towards my future achievements to become more self-confident. The one thing that I thought I did well and enjoyed doing was loving people or showing concern for others.

The concern I showed for others was two-fold for me. I felt like a rock star; ultimately, it gave me worth, and I felt like I had something valuable to offer. Being concerned for others also made me feel like I was walking my purpose. I mean, it gave me complete satisfaction, whether it cost me something or not. Nevertheless, when people disappointed me or said negative things about me, I was sent into an emotional hole, a secret only I and some friends knew of and only food comforted.

I remember one spring afternoon, I was getting ready to go out. I headed to the bus stop to catch the Vaughan 77 (the only bus in Woodbridge at that time that took you past a mall in the Vaughan area, and the local subway station, during my youth). The bus stop to get the Vaughan 77 was at least twenty mins away from my home if travelling on the regular streets, so I used to take a shortcut and walk through a green nature trail. This route reduced my walking time by half. On this day, while walking to the bus stop, I passed a man, and I am quite sure I said hi to him, as this is a normal occurrence for me.

His response to me was, "Hi" followed by, "What kind of disability do you have?"

"I don't have a disability," I responded quickly.

"But your limp?" was his rebuttal. This conversation has never left my mind and has been an additional burden in my life since I participated in it. I would think, *I have never been called disabled before. He doesn't even know me. How could he make such a comment? Am I disabled? Is there something wrong with me? Maybe this was why people have always treated me differently?*

Despite being haunted by these thoughts and feeling them for most of my life, I was always smiling, everywhere…at church, work, school, and home. If I wasn't fighting with them, I was smiling. Looking back, maybe this was my defence mechanism against the malicious world I knew so well: fighting, arguments, racism, discrimination, just plain old hatred. Nevertheless, I became conscious of how I was walking that day and became observant of others' facial expressions. This "observation" has stuck with me for years, and I still find myself conscious at times about how people perceive me.

On the other hand, my family knew me as the healthy girl they knew at birth, and they were in no way accepting a diagnosis other than "normal." But the fact was, I was not normal as per the world standards. I was slower in accomplishing physical tasks than my brothers, I tripped more often than they did, walked slower and even had to take breaks as I walked. I would take twice as long as my counterparts to accomplish a task. Regardless, I still did the same task as others would do. And as much as I appreciated the independence my parents taught me when I needed help with some of these tasks, no one was able to help, and this contributed to my resentment and feeling isolated by those I loved the most in this world: my family.

So, I kept on doing, loving, giving…compensating for the resentment I felt, the loneliness, and hurt. I hoped that, by sharing my love and giving people my time, I would search for my own happiness. Contrary to this voice of reason, I felt more betrayal, more isolation and more sadness, and I knew I needed a change . I knew that I could not accomplish this through my own doing, not anymore. For example, when I was twelve years old, I remember helping an older cousin at home. She used to babysit us, my brothers and me, when my parents worked. One time, I commented on something that she did not agree with and, in her anger, she yelled, "I wish you died in the coma." Although I do not remember the details, I will never forget the hurt I felt when she uttered those words directly to my face. Another example that I vaguely remember took place after work one evening (I worked at a parttime job in a telecommunications company). That evening, I was leaving the office building and felt some excruciating pain in my foot. It was also winter time, and slush was everywhere. I called home to see if I could get a ride, but my phone call was being passed from one individual to another on the other end. Needless to say, I took the bus home that night. In my frustration and pain, while riding the bus, I talked to God, and I asked Him why I had to suffer so much, and how is it that things were made worse in my suffering? I had no one around me to show love towards me. Little did I know that He, Jesus, would introduce His love towards me in an intimate way.

I feel like I need to explain my personality a little. I am and have always been a tenderhearted person. I always felt like this nature of self was less than acceptable, especially since my home was not the sentimental type. So, I was mostly, hiding my true self for fear that I would not be received well. This is also why most of my tears were shed alone…in my room with the light off…on the street while I was waiting for the bus and so forth. I did this so that I would not be criticized for being emotional as this would exasperate the hurt I felt even more. When I did cry before family members, I was quickly hushed and told that I was being irrational.

I have many stories confirming to me that I was only tolerated by people, my family included. Telling them how I felt always ended with them laughing at me, or they were totally insensitive to my needs because they thought I was overly emotional and sensitive. To them, my feeling was misplaced and overly exaggerated. They weren't exactly wrong about my sensitivity. But instead of acknowledging my differences and moving on, they laughed or ignored what they could not empathize with, my very valid emotions. As such, I searched my own selfish desires, loving others through action, desiring to be loved and eating to satisfy any other lack that I experienced.

This goal of loving got me into a lot of compromising situations. For instance, I became overly flattered when guys complimented me on my beauty (not by whistling or making gestures towards me, I hated that.) and asking me for my number. Without fail, I would talk to them, give them my number and dated many them, just for the sake of it. Through this, I gained many stalkers, made out with a few, but in the end, I felt worse about myself because I knew they were using me to get what they wanted or desired, ultimately. I felt used. Additionally, it was through God's grace that I did not have sexual intercourse with any of these past boyfriends (and I use this term loosely). Although I came close many times, it was the Lord that installed fear in me and made me see sex more as a spiritual transfer and not only a matter of having fun. And trust me, I had many friends who would try enticing me with sex. It was a wonder why I always stopped the makeout session before it got too far, but I thank God for His grace.

I must also say, it took years and a divine intervention from God to allow me to understand that my family does love me but in their own way. One of the books that I read that helped me come to this understanding was *Five love Languages* by Gary Chapman. This book helped me understand that there are different ways we receive love, and if we are not conscious of how our loved ones (need to) receive love, then they can live year after year—without experiencing true love. There were many other sources that God lead me to that helped me come to this realization. I will not overwhelm you with these facts now. The effects of not feeling true love has left a scar but also made me more conscious and super aware of the love of God (the greatest love story of my life) It's awesome that He knows us so well that He is aware of our love languages and loves us in the manner that matters the most to us and even beyond our wildest imagination, which allows us to experience true love. One of the verses that stuck with me through my youth was Psalms 27:10 (King James Version): "When my mother and father forsake me, then the Lord will take me up." This verse has led me to appreciate the Lord as my loving Saviour and to see Him as the One that I desperately need. I do not and cannot regret any of my history because it developed me into the person I am now and made me aware of the greatest love. Roman 8:28 (KJV) says, "And we know that all things work together for good to them that love God, to them who are the called, according to His purpose." My relationship with Christ Jesus is stronger because of my endurance in trusting Him in times of emotional need. Amen.

CHAPTER 5

Grace displayed in faith

After a few months of working at the group home, the idea of continuing my education came to my mind. *But how could I possibly be thinking about this? Remember my experience when applying for college?* Your mind can be such a deceitful thing if you don't take control of it. All I knew for sure was that I wanted to help those dealing with mental health issues and even envisioned starting a business that catered to a person's holistic health, as I have dealt with this reality myself. My job at the group home was not providing me this opportunity nor was there any likelihood for this area to be developed in the future by staying there. So, while I worked at the group home, I started researching universities and visiting some, as well, with friends from the human service counselling program.

One thing I knew for sure, as I looked for universities, was that I wanted to move away from home. At this point, I believe that I knew my family loved me but the majority of the time I did not feel supported or loved by them in the ways that mattered to me. I often felt like I was getting in the way of their happiness. Because of this unhappiness, I would often sneak away, hide and eat.

Food, as I have stated, remained an outlet for me especially when I felt lonely…it was always there when I needed it the most! One day as I was reading my Bible, I remember a chapter and verse stood out to me, Genesis 12:1,2:

> Now the LORD said to Abram, 'Go forth from your country, and from your relatives and from your father's house, To the land which I will show you; And I will make you a great nation, And I will bless you, And make your name great; And so you shall be a blessing.

I had no idea what this scripture meant at the time, but I knew that this verse resonated with me as I felt like I needed a change.

Throughout my search, only two universities stood out to me, for one reason or another, the University of Windsor and University of Calgary. Originally, I applied for both, but soon the University of Calgary required more information from me and the task became tedious and annoying. I grew weary. After going back and forth a few times with this university, I felt as if what they were requiring of me was monotonous, and I stopped communicating with them. My hope was now solely on the response of the admission team at the University of Windsor. The waiting drove me crazy but within a few weeks, I heard back, and it was great news—I was accepted. I couldn't believe this transition had been so easy for me this time. I was going to university despite the disbelief and doubts of my past teachers, those around me, and (sadly some of the doubts came from) me. I had become too familiar with the negative talks in my surroundings, and soon I would be away from that.

Prior to being accepted to Windsor University, my church had had a youth convention. What I remember the most was a prophecy that was given to me by the guest speaker. This guest speaker was from America, and he did not know me, nor did I know him, but one night from his altar he pointed me out in the crowd of youth and prophesied that I will be by rivers of water and that I will be used by God. This prophesy struck me in a way that is hard to explain, but when I went home that night to look up where the University of Windsor was located, and guess what I noted? It was right beside the Detroit River.

This was fascinating to me and brought me great joy and reassurance. Because of the prophecy, I became more aware that God was in this process. Oh, I forgot to mention that the course I got accepted into at Windsor University (which had an outstanding reputation for their social work program), was the PreSocial Work Program, which was used to narrow down the most eligible applicants for the bachelor program, thus ensuring they had passionate and dedicated students. Nevertheless, my initial admission would not guarantee that I would be a candidate for the post social work program. When I got to the orientation, 300 people were looking to be promoted to the Post-Social Work Program. Despite the pressure, I felt assured that God had placed me there, and I did not worry about what the future held for me at this school.

I remember the feelings of accomplishment and gratitude when I received my first test back; it was in one of my women's study classes. I got an A, and to celebrate, I called my mother in

Toronto to brag about my achievement. Initially, I felt refreshed being in Windsor…away from the hurt I once knew…it was as if Windsor signified a rebirthing process for me. This was my chance to be redeemed from all I knew of…the hurt and betrayal. Soon, Windsor became a lonely place for me to live. After a week, I quickly noticed that, although I was away from those that hurt me emotionally, in Windsor, I was physically alone. I didn't know what was worse, feeling alone among those you love or actually being alone. Regardless of the loneliness, I always describe Windsor as the place where my major spiritual growth took place.

I drew closer to God…And He began to reintroduce Himself to me in a new way. I had no distractions, and soon enough my relationship with Christ grew intimate. One of my first heartfelt conversations with God was about my weight. By the time I got to university, I weighed 119 Kg (264 lbs) and wore size 24. With my size and limp, walking to school was no walk in the park and school was only 6-10 minutes away from my dorm. I remember having breathing difficulties, and the immersing pain walking to school and even from class to class. It was very rare for me to communicate as I walked, and I remember stopping a couple of times during my walk to school to gasp air and gain strength for the remainder of the walk; I never seemed to have enough air in my lungs.

One day I went outside my dorm to talk to God, and in this prayer, I relayed to God that I knew that He has put so much in me to give and do, but I wasn't sure if I could do it all because of what I was experiencing physically. I went on to say that I was ready and willing to do His will (something I often said to God), but I needed more endurance and physical ability to accomplish

His will. I am not sure how long it took, but all I know is that in the course of my four years in Windsor, I lived and exercised with people who loved to exercise and knew how to eat proper meals.

By the time I graduated, I had lost over 27 Kg (60 lbs), and I also started going to a physiotherapist. I felt healthier. Coincidentally, this was not the only a portion of blessings that God's poured on me during my stay in Windsor. I felt like our relationship was based on His faithfulness towards me despite my humanity. I vividly remember times where He would wake me up at 5 a.m. in the morning and would speak to me through His Word or moments when He provided a financial miracle. There were days, after praying to God about my fears of not having, when I would I check my bank account, and nothing was there. The next morning, I found enough money for what I needed from a grant I had applied for or from my mother without me telling her I needed it. God is great.

Aside from all of this, another great blessing that God did for me was to introduce me to fellow Christians on campus. Varsity Christian Warriors was a group on campus that provided me with friendship during a time of isolation as well as providing me the opportunity to develop my spiritual growth with likeminded people. Many of us began to worship with each other but Zakiyia, a group member within the Varsity Christian Warrior—she embraced me and was the first person to take me around Windsor, and Detroit, to look for a home church. Before meeting Zakiyia, I would relax in my room and watch sermons on my computer…I didn't have a television to call my own. Despite this, I found that God would answer me, even though the ministries I watch on my computer. Nonetheless, there is a different level of power and peace when you are able to worship with people, rather than watch it on TV. The Bible declares in Matthew 18:20 (KJV), "For where two or three are gathered together in my name, there am I in the midst of them."

The process of meeting likeminded people meant so much to me and aided in teaching me so much about my relationship with Christ. They (Varsity Christian Warriors) also challenged me to step out of my comfort zone and become bolder, by encouraging me to present five-minute messages to the group (all would participate in this activity). This was a giant step for me...having grown up in my father's church; the idea of speaking in public placed such a fear in me. I remember situations when I spoke before the congregation, which would result in me trembling from head to toe...and what made the experience even worse was my voice. It would tremble but and getting a full sentence out was almost impossible.

Another memorable blessing was after being selected as one of the students who would be moving on to the actual Bachelor of Social Work program. I meet some friends along the way. Some of which are now long lasting friendships. One day I met a friend named Jen; she is a sweetheart. From the moment we met, we began calling one another sister, She invited me to her birthday party and obviously, I wanted to go because after meeting Jen, she appeared to have a sweet genuine spirit...but because I was brought up in a legalistic church I was torn and wondered if I would be betraying my Christianity if I went to her party. She wasn't a born again Christian. Tormented, I spoke to God about it. In this conversation with God, I asked, "Can't I just have fun?" I wanted to go and support my new friend. I am not certain if I gave a proposition to God but as I write this, I can imagine myself having said, "Maybe I can be a light and be the difference you want me to be in the midst of darkness." What I do remember is the response to my question, and it happened days later.

At that time, I had found and was consistently going to a church in Detroit. This particular night I attended a Bible study. Afterwards, I greeted a few people and was about to put my jacket on to leave when a lady greeted me, "I don't know why, but I feel the Lord wants me to tell you that, you can have fun." Shut the front door! God being God, took time to answer my literal prayer. I said thanks to the lady (with a confused look on my face), wished her well, went to my car and cried all the way home. I could not believe that God, so mighty, so grandeur, would be so engaged and concerned about a problem I had, something that others would consider so small and minute.

It was these small encounters with God that had the greatest impact on me and gave me a longing to seek him more wholeheartedly. But this did not come without challenges. Being away from home also afforded me a lot of worldly attributes and increased my curiosity. Many of the roommates that I had while away weren't Christians…many had sexual exploits with random men which awakened a sexual inquisitiveness in me or dealt with alcoholism problems which opened my eyes to self-loathing and others that dealt with their own self-esteem issues. I am not saying that Christians do not encounter these issues, they do. But the more mature you become in Christ these issues should become non-existent. For me, these situations were a shock to me since I was never introduced or exposed to these things growing up. One of the first houses I lived in, once I moved out of the dorm, was owned by a woman named Kelly. The best landlord I can remember…. She would rent rooms of the homes she owned near campus.

When renting, I would also look for a room in a house, but that meant that I wouldn't know who my roommates would be until I moved in. Many of these roommates introduced me to a life that I was not accustomed to. Sonia, one of my first roommates, introduced me to the effects of alcoholism. Many times, she would go out and get drunk, and then come home in a drunken stupor; she would end up either passed out on the lawn or yelling or pounding on the house door at 3 a.m. Many times I would drag her to the bathroom to shower her off (with her clothes on) to help her sober up.

Another set of friends included those I most regularly went to church with when travelling in Detroit. This was not a regular routine for those living in Windsor, but it was a church that I liked attending since I was introduced to it. One day we, my friends and I, went shopping in Detroit, which happened more regularly than anything else in Windsor. This trip came with a shocking surprise. I had left my bag in the shopping cart as I shopped, but at some point during my scavenging, when I looked into my cart, my bag was gone. I panicked. I did everything that I could do. I retraced my steps, went out to the car to see if I had left it there, spoke to the security. Nothing. I lost my identification, my money (over 400 dollars), my makeup (I'm talking about Clinque makeup, y'all) and more. How was I going to get back into Canada? How was I going to access my money or go to my medical appointments? Fortunately, when we got to the border, the border security officer was nice enough to let me and my friends cross after hearing this horrible story. Trisha, one of my friends on the trip offered to take me to Toronto one weekend, as she had already planned, to get all my documents back.

After our four hour trip to Toronto and on our way back to Windsor…I informed Trisha of the experience I had in Toronto and the money I had to pay to attain all of my documents again. Maybe I was wrong, in thinking about it now, but when she dropped me off at my house, I said thanks and told her how much I appreciated her driving me but did not give her any money to compensate her for the journey and gas used.

In my defence, I had so much on my mind, and I didn't think of it at the time. But within a week I heard some people gossiping about me, and it wasn't pleasant. I complained about how I was being treated to the only person I felt would listen…my mom, and also God. My parents decided to buy me a car. They arrived in Windsor, unannounced. What a surprising and thoughtful gesture. This gesture was a shock to me because I was not accustomed to this loving outpour from my parents. Don't we all do this though, take advantage and ignore what we have until it's gone? This gesture proved my parents love for me despite their humanity, which did not always make me feel accepted or respected. I was amazed and so very grateful at the same time. This was my time to be fully independent. God is so good to me!

Some of my other experiences in Windsor were more invasive, like hearing my roommates having sexual encounters with men, but the curiosity of the sexual pleasures I heard night after night had lasting effects on me mentally. As a result, there were occasions where I would masturbate in the shower, and whenever I got the chance to. This was something I had never done for a quarter of my life. And I was ashamed, but it became my reality, and regardless of the guilt and repentant attitude that I had, this habit continued for some time, years even. I was consumed by guilt during this period. I knew that this particular action disappointed

God and that He called me to live at a higher standard, to live a pure life before him. I did my best to ignore this habit that I adopted, I continued to go to church, spend time with friends and attend a local Bible study close to my home. But the truth is, I acted as if I was innocent of any wrong, little did I know then, but realize now, that peoples' opinion of me still had a great impact on my life and thus, I kept this action a secret.

I knew if I would do anything for Christ, I had to become vulnerable and fully surrendered towards Him, allowing God to fine tune me. Like I said, this habit continued for years but on the down low of course. I mean I had a reputation to uphold. My whole identity was attached to the church; this is where I was raised. The church provided me a particular freedom from the accusations I received from the world around me. I was being judged for everything else, and I did want the habit of masturbation to become my new vice.

So, I continued to hide this habit, pray about it and claim healing for it. But the truth is that it continued occurring.

It wasn't until I return to Toronto and found a home church that I started to share my struggles with masturbation and begin to surrender to Christ on another level. But before this act of surrender happened I remember that the continuous act of masturbation started to make me feel nauseated and ill. I am not sure why this happened, but it certainly didn't hinder me from my selfish act. But God is good despite my humanity. One day, I began listening to sermons and in these particular sermons, spoke about deliverance. This sermon alluded me to look to Jesus and not be consumed by what I have to do or accomplish. He, Jesus comes and delivers you. This is what happened to me, I stopped striving and simply looked up. I consumed myself for months with songs of praise, listened to messages, and I stopped watching shows that would erect a feeling or sensation in me that was counterintuitive. My day was literally seventy percent God and thirty percent everything else…I had to be purposeful now in all that I did. And it was my pursuit for Christ that help me to overcome this debilitating habit.

Only God knew what was ahead for me. After graduating university, living independently for several years and finding a good family church in Windsor, was all I needed, and as such, I had no intentions of moving back to Toronto. I was content. Toronto was a place I associated with emotional pain and heartache, a place where I felt the most physical pain. But God new otherwise. A few months after graduating, the economy in Windsor crashed, and regardless of my education or the effort I placed in finding jobs, I could not find a job anywhere. I even tried applying to other countries like Scotland but with it came unrealistic restrictions, restrictions that dictated that expats must apply to the international job recruitment agencies within a certain timeframe.

So, due to the age restrictions (I was considered a mature student at the age of twenty-nine). This meant I was too old (Too old! How rude!) to transfer to Scotland for work. Moreover, I had quit my part-time job as a personal support worker, a job I had during school, even though it placed a lot of unwarranted physical discomfort on me. I had kept that job because I didn't feel like I had a choice I needed the extra money, but after graduating, I didn't have to tolerate this job any more, which is why I couldn't wait to quit. My hope was that I could find something in my new field.

My hopes to stay in Windsor became less of a possibility and slowly, it became hard for me to maintain my independence. Soon, I started using the food bank at my church in Windsor—concealed from friends and definitely my roommates so that the money I had could pay for rent and bills. My mother hated hearing me suffer and would send money when she could, and God used her to give during the most desperate times, without me even saying a word.

She began mentioning the option of moving back home, but this was not the dream I had for myself, and neither was it apart of the prophecy I had years ago, so how could it be God's plan for me? So, I persisted, until I could no longer do so. I kept wondering, *How could I return to a place that hurt me emotionally and prevented me from living authentically?*

A decision had to be made, and, eventually, when nothing else seemed to line up for me, I moved back home, reluctantly.

When I thought about moving back to Toronto, I would wonder, *What will living back in Toronto look like? Where will I go to church? How long will I stay at home before moving out on my own again? Would my feelings change once I lived there?* I had so many uncertainties, but what I knew for sure was that I didn't want to resort to my old ways. I knew that God had changed me and made me more confident than I was before, and I had no intentions of going back.

When I began considering my move, the first thing I needed to look after was all the belongings I had accumulated over the four or five years in my beloved city, Windsor. After considering the cost, struggles and the challenges I endured to obtain some of my belongings, I thought it would be best to move most of my belonging to Toronto. Of course, to accomplish this, I knew

I would need help. So, I called home to see if I would have help transporting by belongings. That night, I felt as I once did many years ago, when I lived at home. My call was passed from person to another. Again, I found myself feeling rejected and unloved… as my family's answer was a resounding no! No one could help with the move.

So, I looked into a moving company to assist me, but the cost was more than what I could handle financially, and when I called my father for financial help, he informed me that he did not have the money to lend me. The move was not yet finalized, but I was beginning to feel neglected and unwanted as I had years before.

Many doubts flooded my mind, but the most consistent thought was, *Is this truly the best thing for me?* Convinced by my mother, I sold most of what I had and even lost money in the process because of the time constraints. The smaller items that I could not sell would come back with me to Toronto. So, I packed up my car and headed home.

I have always loved driving, and the longer I drove the better. Long drives meant that I could sing, I could dance in my seat, I could act according to my own standards without being judged, and most importantly, it was my time to speak to Jesus while being away from everyone and any noise.

Driving represented true freedom for me, and I was grateful for the blessing of my car. Accordingly, my drive back to Toronto was a peaceful one, one where I experienced the peace and joy that I always experienced when I got into my car. My prayer as I drove to my parents' home that day was for God to guide and strengthen me as I took this leap of faith. I would never have fathomed the road that was ahead, now living back in the city where I once grew up in.

CHAPTER 6

Shelter in the storm

It probably won't shock you to hear that I was not thrilled to be back in Toronto because I knew that this time around, it would not be like one of my short visits, like my many visits to Toronto from Windsor. But something in me wanted to adjust as best as possible to my reassigned habitation and just trust God, as I have done so many times in the past.

I wasted no time in getting myself settled when I arrived and as soon as possible I began applying for jobs. In my parent's home, work and an accumulation of financial security gave you significance, a sense of worth. This was now my priority. I went to different employment centre's, applying for ten to fifteen jobs a day. I got many interviews due to my diligence in applying for jobs. I would assume that I had four to five interviews a month, soon these interviews became tedious and overwhelming because they did not lead to anything promising. At times, I became really frustrated when I did not get the response I was looking for from positions I really thought I was qualified for. With this frustration and the discouragement of living back home.

I noticed that I started gaining some weight back. Oh no! This was not something I wanted. Food again was becoming a clutch for me, in my frustration. I believed that a part of the freedom I experienced in Windsor was due to being healthier and able to accomplish more. Unfortunately, realizing the weight gain happened at a later time, which meant I wore one dress size larger. Although this may not look like much, it equates to gaining 15 to 20 lbs. So, as often as I could I worked out at home until I could do better. I was now juggling maintaining my weight and looking for work while prepping for interviews. Hard work was never some that had deterred me in the past, and it would not deter me now. After 7 months of searching, I landed a job at Ontario March of Dimes as an independent living resource worker.

I remember the day I had my interview. I was nervous, especially because the interviews I had before always ended with a rejection for one reason or another. This time around, I equipped myself with the words of God…Psalms 23 to be exact!

> The Lord is my shepherd;
> I shall not want.
> He makes me to lie down in green pastures;
> He leads me beside the still waters.
> He restores my soul;
> He leads me in the paths of righteousness
> For His name's sake.
>
> Yea, though I walk through the valley
> of the shadow of death,

I will fear no evil;
For You are with me;
Your rod and Your staff, they comfort me.

You prepare a table before me in the presence
of my enemies;
You anoint my head with oil;
My cup runs over.
Surely goodness and mercy shall follow me
All the days of my life;
And I will dwell in the house of the Lord
Forever.

After reading this chapter of Psalms, I kept repeating the first few words to myself, "The Lord is my shepherd, I shall not want" until I heard my name called. I met with two people that day and was convinced that one interviewer was interested in me while the other showed no interest in me at all during the interview.

Afterwards, I left there thinking, *It's in the Lord's hands now.* It was perhaps two weeks later that I got the call from Ontario March of Dimes; they wanted to hire me for the job. Hallelujah! My official day of work would be on December 21, 2008.

Before I began working, my mother surprised me with a trip to Jamaica (a graduation gift). I was so excited to travel as it was a much need vacation, and to make things more exciting, my friend from elementary school, Donna, and her baby daughter Laurilee, travelled with us as well. Throughout our trip, we stayed with my uncle's in Brownstown, Jamaica, the town both my mother and uncle grew up in. We would travel back and forth to Ocho Rios to visit the many different beaches, Bob Marley's house in St. Ann, and many more places.

One of the places that my mother mentioned she wanted me to visit was Dunn's River Falls. My mother said that these waters had healing properties and that by putting my feet in, I could receive healing for an injury that I had had for more than a quarter of my life, the difficulty I had endured since the coma. Being both desperate and having faith in a miraculous God, I believed that He could use anything to heal. I was more than willing to try it.

Dunn's River Falls had blue-green water. The glorious sun shone on me as I looked beyond the beach. Seeing and hearing the tourists walking up the falls with their tour guides and experiencing the gust of the rains that came from the falls in the background of where I stood was an experience in itself. At the bottom of the Dunn's River Falls was a ring of water. I stood surrounded by boulders. As I stood in the warm water which covered my feet, my mother splashed the water on different parts of my legs.

"Do you feel any difference?" my mother repeated. I was unsure how to reply to that question considering I had my feet planted in the water for forty-five minutes but had a lifetime of pain in my legs, and feet. This question was hard for me to answer because I had many experiences where I would feel pain in my feet and then, miraculously, regain strength in them after a few days.

At some point, I got tired of standing in the water and decided that my healing would come when God willed it to. What I wanted at that moment was to join Donna and Laurilee on the beach and enjoy the intoxication of beauty before me. When I did, we enjoyed the ocean together walking, swimming, splashing and sitting in the shallow beginnings of the sea-green waters and then having the privilege of sunbathing on the beach (yes, I love to sun bathe). As we relaxed on the beach, we could hear the motor of many skidoos out on the water. And our curiosity was piqued, or maybe I should say mine was. I wanted to try something new.

I got up from lying on the beach, walked towards the ocean, and got the attention of one of the men who was giving ski-dooing lessons on the beach that day. I must admit I was a bit scared to take on an activity such as this one, not only because was I poor swimmer but my physical restraints have somewhat limited me in the past but like I have said before, persistence had become my second nature. It was the reality of Christ's word and promises that have always propelled me to try and persist. And if I thought there was a possibility for me to perform a task I would try to do it despite my limitation. "Mike" persuaded me to ride with him while promising to take me to see the water arena and to see a pod of dolphins that were on the other side of Dunn's River. With butterflies in my stomach, I agreed to Mike's proposition. I should add that my mother was more nervous than I was in me trying this activity and pleaded with Mike to keep me safe. Again, if there was one thing that I have learned is that with Christ all things are possible, and thus far, this promise has been a reality for me.

What a fantastic time I had that day, the wind blowing through my hair, excitement and nervousness running through my mind and heart. I saw dolphins that day but not as closely as promised. Regardless, I was reminded of the peace that comes from trusting in the Creator and His perfect plan for you.

Along with this, there were many things that I did in Jamaica that I didn't know that I could physically do, like when I climbed a steep hill to meet my grandfather for what seemed to be the first time. I had met my grandfather as a child. I was maybe two or three years old, but I do not remember that experience at all. I mean, I knew I loved him and, in fact, we would also chat with each other on occasions when my mother called him or vice versa. We would chat and dream about one day meeting each other.

I remember my visit with my grandfather so well. He was ninety five at the time, in good health, physically, but was considered legally blind. My visit with him consisted of him serenading us all, Donna and me massaging his feet, having him feeling my face, arms and legs (this helped him to get an idea of how I looked), and watching him comb his hair. He took great pride in his appearance.

We chatted about the possibility of him coming to visit us in Toronto and spoke about the different excursions I would take him on, which included going to the harbourfront and taking a boat ride together. There, he could feel the cool breeze brush against his cheeks. We had such a good time together, and for a minute I did not feel apprehensive about how I would be received and felt loved for who I was. I was truly grateful and cherished the moments my grandfather and I had together.

Sadly, after meeting my grandfather and making several plans together, he died a few months after our trip. I was confused and shocked. Why did I lose my grandfather so quickly, especially since we had a chance to rekindle our relationship and planned to spend time with one another? Why did I have to lose someone I had so much faith in, already? My mother and I could not afford to go back to Jamaica together since we were there only three months before. So, my mother went without me. I had some regrets about not going back but only God knew why.

Fortunately, I had my new job to look forward to and to prepare for, which occupied my thoughts. I wanted to do an excellent job and as a trained social worker, my concern was effectively meeting the needs of my new clients. Consequently, I set a high standard for myself and was critical of myself when I fell beneath my status quo. Now that I think of it, I needed to prove to myself that I was competent, worthwhile of the role that I was now playing.

When I think back, I was grateful and blessed to have gained a job working at Ontario March of Dimes. I felt as if this job provided me opportunities for growth in my skills but also as a person. My supervisor and the central team helped me in this growth process. They took the time to know and appreciate me for me. I really felt this way and when I needlessly apologized for something that I messed up in, they (especially my supervisor) reminded me that I was human and, as such, we all make mistakes. My supervisor was great at complimenting me for my efforts and would also give me leniency to think outside of the box. Because of his guidance, as a true leader, I was able to create a community building event and took part in several activities that I considered to be above my pay grade at the time. My supervisor invested in his team and in many ways, it helped me to trust the process God created for me.

On top of this, I loved my clients—all of them. They were special and unique in many ways. They all suffered from some sort of physical disability, ranging from Cerebral Palsy to being quadriplegic. They were so kind hearted, regardless that they all needed financial, social, governmental, and some, mental, assistance. My job mainly was to help these individuals find housing, but once they found accommodations in our building sites, my role became that of a case manager, and I would assist them in their day-to-day. So, whether they needed help with coping daily or needed some more help from government funding, I would try my best to assist them. I loved my job. I loved learning about new aspects of my job, I loved communicating with my clients, beginning new groups, associating with other groups and businesses in the local area. I loved it all. There was also an element of newness that came with my job. I never knew what to expect in the day, as things would arise as the day went by. Many times, I found myself on the road travelling from one site to the other or from one organization to the next. Time went so fast, as you could imagine, and before I knew it, I was in my role for almost three years.

I loved my job, but it came with some strenuous situations, as all jobs do. I began feeling worn out. I started noticing that I was beginning to feel ill in the morning before I started my work day. My travel to work was becoming stressful in itself, and many times I found myself praying that God would provide me with access to a bathroom or with the ability to control my bladder as I travelled to work. It became the norm to stop off from the highway or in between my travel to and from my worksites to use the bathroom. I also noticed small periods of sever pain in my ankles and feet, which alarmed me. In addition to all of this, I began noticing political issues in my job, one that affected me personally.

As I mentioned before, my key role as a resource worker at the Ontario March of Dimes was to get people with disabilities into supportive housing. Without getting into much detail, due to confidentiality reasons and loyalty to my past employment, an assessment is taken to determine the eligibility for one particular client, which ended up with racial slurs being directed to my colleague and myself. The result of this harassment shocked the very core of who I was and caused me to lose hope in a system I once believed in. With all of this said, I still loved the role that I played.

It was the end of October 2011, and I felt confronted with making a choice: to work for Christ or to continue to work for man, community, society or this particular organization. I believe that God was ultimately causing me to choose between working for a humanistic standard or rising above it. Living through His status quo. I am going to pause here for a while. I know that many people would disagree with my last statement. I mean why would a just God give His children an ultimatum? Rightfully so, I cannot answer this, but what I can do is relay the experience I had.

This ultimatum brought me to tears. I felt as if I was in a tug-of-war. On one side stood Christ and on the other stood my financial security. I even remember going to my supervisor and asking him for a leave of absence instead of resigning…I mean I wanted to be obedient to God's call, but I also wanted to feel comfortable in doing so. But God would not allow it. My supervisor informed me that the government was implementing a new standardized intake procedure and because of it I was not allowed to take a leave of absence. Again, I found myself at a crossroad and had to make, what I felt, a serious decision. I proceeded back to my office, sat at my desk and wrote out a resignation letter, and it went something like this:

Dear So and So,

Regrettably, I would like to submit to you my resignation letter. I would like to thank you for all the opportunity found in this position. It was my hope to take a leave of absence from this position to explore other avenues and volunteer as a life skill facilitator, but because I was denied the chance to take a leave of absence, I have decided to resign.

I hope that you can understand my decision, and I wish Ontario March of Dimes all the success for the near future.

Lorraine Parke

Each key that I typed was a difficult one. I could not cease from thinking about my security or lack thereof. After I typed up this letter, I took a breath and uttered, "OK, God, it is you and me now, and I am trusting you for tomorrow."

I went home that evening not scared but determined to bring my dreams to life, but it didn't come without a struggle.

My family thought I was crazy and were not a hundred per cent certain about my decision. They kept wondering if another option could have been made. Maybe I could have explored my dreams while I was working…I tried explaining the experience I had encountered in my office, but the more I explained, the more they refuted, and so I stopped after some time. While this practical transition was going on, researching how to start a business and developing life skill workshops, another one (mentally) was taking place as well. So many things were happening.

I came back from Windsor, my grandpa whom I loved passed, I was attending a church where I felt I could not be myself and more.

Although I saw glimpses of joy, overall, there was not much to be happy about. In fact, I remember having an episode during this time, in my car. And it happened after attending, my now former church, while I was driving home from church. That Sunday, I cried. I did not fully understand why I was crying, but it was one of those heart wrenching cries. It was as if I had a physical hole in my heart, and I literally felt air going through it and this was not the only time. Like I said, most of these cries happened driving home from church, which gave me the opportunity to speak to God in private and hear from Him as well.

I would ask Him, *why am I so sad? So empty? Especially since I heard from you during service?* It was clear to me that I needed to do some soul searching and fast, which for me meant spending time with God, hearing His voice and listening to praise music. I would get things done in the day but in the evening, I locked myself in my room to spend needed time with my Father. I did this for about a month.

Meanwhile, I registered my business, wrote a business plan with assistance, developed a few lesson plans and landed a volunteer opportunity with Salvation Army facilitating a nine week course on employability. These lessons were developed by yours truly, and when I presented the course to the manager, he didn't hesitate. A week later, I was facilitating.

I was so elated! I had an extra pep in my step. I was making a difference, an imprint in the sand.

Many times, I stayed back because someone needed an ear or advice about something. This was it. I was in my niche, not getting paid for it but I saw myself in this realm. I was doing exactly what I was meant to do and so much satisfaction came from knowing that I was making a difference. My commute was 31.5 Km or 26-30 minutes depending on traffic and would take place every Monday evening. My group started at 7 p.m. Imagine, being in the middle of heavy traffic but being in total peace! This, in itself, was a miracle!

There were times I had up to fifteen people in attendance; it was so successful that I was asked to expand my lesson plan for an extra two weeks. When this opportunity ended, I began searching for my next facilitation opportunity and began developing several lesson plans on topics that catered to time management, conflict resolution, selfesteem, bullying, effective communication, dealing with stress and so forth. I was never an avid reader growing up, but in this period of my life, I was buying numerous books on Amazon and reading them within weeks to prepare for my potential groups, even though I had no confirmed bookings.

Nevertheless, I wanted to be sure that I was being current and giving people updated and relevant information. I began writing blogs as well, on topics that would assist a person in their wellness while providing subjective experiences as well. From the beginning, it was important for me to incorporate my life skill programs with my Christian values because, in my opinion, it was these two things that assisted me in overcoming many of my anxiety issues. It was the exploration and research of many life skills books that allowed me to see the many connections between the Word of God and the books I read. God's desire for us is to be whole. Reading these life skill books clarified to me that the Bible is full of instructions that cater to one's holistic well-being, and you need not look any further.

For me, I could not separate the two and would read my life skill books while studying the Word of God and saw many familiarities.

Many of my past blogs also incorporated scriptures that were relevant to the topics presented. I got some responses to my blogs and even saw some private clients, but it was nothing to brag about. Eventually, I found my spirit getting weaker and my hope dissipating. Nevertheless, I noticed that God always sent me a word or provided a situation that would encourage me during this exasperating time and as such, I kept my business active. Accordingly, God opened doors and would allow me clients that were sufficient enough for me to work in my business on a parttime basis.

One Friday night after going to the gym, I visited a church, New Life Christian Centre to be exact. I remember the first time like it was yesterday. I was a bit late arriving, due to the fact I was trying to get my mom to visit with me; nevertheless, when I arrived, the praise and worship team was singing, and again I found myself in tears.

This time around, though, my tears represented more gratefulness and gratitude for a God that has done so much for me, even with disappointment. From this moment on, I was drawn to NLCC but was still faithful towards my obligations at the church I was attending then. Soon, I found myself going to fulfill my obligations at one church and attending another because I was being drawn to it. After a few weeks of going back and forth, I spoke to God and told him that I didn't want to live out a confused life. I wanted to be dedicated to one church only, and because I knew God was not the author of confusion, I knew I didn't need to invite confusion into my life. After our conversation,

I went on a fast for my answer. I fasted for three weeks, and it was not a typical fast. I ate food as regular but I wasn't going to watch television or go on social media; instead, I would read my Bible, do devotions and immerse myself in worship music, and I did just that.

After the end of my fast, I knew God was talking to me about authenticity. He wanted me to step into a realm where I knew who I was in Christ, and to stop living a life where I was more concerned with what people thought of me. He was pushing me a little further. That night I decided that I leave the church I was attending, despite my title and role at the church, and begin attending New Life Christian Church.

I was so scared. I mean, I had responsibilities at the church, and I did not want to hurt anyone in the process, but I new what I had to do. So, the Sunday after my fast, I went to church as normal and listened to the message the pastor delivered. The pastor confirmed to me what God was saying to me in my spirit for the past month. He spoke about authenticity that day, and I knew God provided me with that word to encourage me to overcome my fears. Still timid, I spoke to the pastor of that church that day and told him what I felt. The pastor discussed my decision with me but asked that I think about staying and concluded by suggesting we touch base in the week. I did see him later that week to continue our conversation. Thankfully, we came to the agreement that I would help out for an additional week and then part ways. And being a woman of my word, I did.

I never stopped going to New Life Christian Centre from the day I started. That Friday evening, my eyes were opened to something new. Something new? You may be asking, "What do you mean by that?" Well, it took a while for me to comprehend the way I was feeling after I started attending.

I loved the Word of God, I love the atmosphere there, and I love those I meet. Do you see a theme? Love. Authentic love. It didn't matter where I came from, I was accepted for my eclectic personality. It felt as if I had been to this church for decades before and many of the new friendships that I cultivated there appeared as lifelong relationships. Nevertheless, after about a week of attending this church on a fulltime basis, I lost the ability to continue driving my car.

Confused, I asked God, "Why did you allow this to happen?" As I stated previously, my car was not only my access to independence, but it also represented peace for me. I began wondering how I would get around for my business and get to church regularly. But God knew more than I did. I have never had friends, strangers at that time, rally around me and help me so much. I had rides when I needed them, provision for things, and given money without me even asking. Let me pause here to give another testimony. During this time, a good friend of mine, a past classmate and ex-roommate, was getting married. And I had the privileged to participate in her joyous occasion. I was excited for her and wanted to give her a gift that she deserved but didn't have the cash to buy her something I thought she deserved. So, I began talking to God about it and shared my frustration with him. I was frustrated because there was an obvious strain in my finances, I was working part-time through my business, I no longer had the ability to get to as many clients as I desired because I lost my car, and I wasn't able to find another longer-term facilitation job due to my immobility. But I did not want this to hinder the support I gave to my friend during this occasion. My prayer and concerns went up to God continually, and I didn't tell my frustrations to another human being.

At the same time, a sister in Christ at NLCC was having a lot of anxiety, and we both agreed that it would be nice if I could spend a couple of weeks with her and her family, to help her through some of the negative thoughts she was having. Daily, we read together, prayed together and had some very intense conversations about her past experiences. I am not sure if I helped her in those couple of weeks, but I know that God spoke to me about His love towards me, through this family. One day, my sister in Christ called me down to her basement to show me a few things she had but hadn't used since her wedding. She asked me if I knew anyone who needed these things, being clueless, which sometimes happens… I said no. After a few more minutes going through her belonging and organizing things, I said to her, "Janet," (this is not her name, but I will use it just they same) "you know what's funny?"

"What?"

"I have a wedding shower that I'm going to on Saturday, and I don't have a gift yet," I responded.

"Lorraine, look at this crystal set of glasses. We have never used them. Why don't you give them as a gift to your friend?"

"Are you sure, Janet?" I replied in disbelief.

"Yes, we will go out and look for something to wrap this gift in. By the time I am done, it will look like new."

"Oh, thank you. I really appreciate this! Can I be excused for a minute?" I am sure you can guess what I did at that moment or maybe not. I went out side, prayed and gave thanks with tears in my eyes. I was so thankful to God for being so involved and concerned about my concerns. I was humbled that a Great God would take time to answer such a basic prayer. Little did I know, but God would reintroduce me to HIS GREAT LOVE. This happened for months…God showed me His love and faithfulness through the acts and kindness of His children.

CHAPTER 7

Enduring pain

There were few days without pain. Sadly enough, pain became a normal occurrence. The only period I recall when my physical pain was not as prominent was the second or third year of university. I started losing weight and attending a physiotherapist. I began feeling better and do not recall many hindrances in my physical attributes. I believed with all my heart that I was walking into my years of restoration. What do you mean by that, Lorraine? Well, I believed that God was healing my sick body and that my desires for my health and wellness were becoming a real occurrence. My testament that He saved me at the age of seventeen (the last time I entered the hospital) and since then, I have never once returned to the hospital. Like the rainbow that was a promise from God to all His children, never to destroy our land again, my personal sign that God would heal my body was his protecting me from further illnesses since I had given my heart to Christ.

Oddly enough, returning to Toronto was when I began enduring more frequent physical pain. Of course, it did not happen right away, but I increased in weight, and without realizing it, the pain became louder than I wanted it to. On a daily basis, I made the decision to tolerate the pain and to continue to do what I was required to do—go to work, church and do family life with a smile on my face.

This was and has always been difficult for me—don't get me wrong, as a Child of God, I still walked with the hope of healing, but there were days where I felt overwhelmed by the pain. Regardless, I kept on fulling my duties, and the pain became second nature to me. Endurance became my second name. Accordingly, the Word of God became my lifeline, and its daily promises provided me hope and gave me encouragement for the days ahead.

I recall one day when I endured immense oral pain. This happened a year or two after I quit my job. What I remember the most is positioning myself in a fetal position on my bed and crying continuously. I called out to God in my distress and stated to Him that I feel trapped. "Lord," I said, "Why do I need to endure such pain? I feel like I am in a box, and all around me is physical and emotional pain, financial distress, and I can't do this anymore. I would rather die." I shared with my mom my distress, and in her eyes, I was being overly dramatic. Because she did not like to see me in such distress, she gave me money to have my wisdom tooth pulled, which was causing the unbearable pain. Although grateful, I became aware that no one could ever understand what I had been enduring. I was truly alone, or so I thought.

God, on the other hand, has always directed my steps, and I am reminded of a verse in Proverbs 3:5, "Trust in the Lord with all of your heart and do not rely on your own understanding."

This passage means a lot to me because I have truly seen the Lord leading me in pain, as I trusted in Him. Take New Life Christian Church, for instance. God led me there and since being a part of this congregation, I have learned what it means to love more authentically and to be content and confident in who God has made me to be. Let me give you insight, and I may be repeating myself, but I feel it is necessary to mention it again. Before coming to New Life Christian Church, I felt condemned most of the time. I felt I was not accepted for my unique attributes and would be referred to by my spiritual family and my own blood relatives as "white" or "different."

Growing up I would be considered more liberal than my colour counterpart. I was brought up in a Jamaican-Canadian home, and a lot of my friends I grew up with in church were black. But I did not act as they did. Maybe this was because I grew up in Woodbridge, and although I was bullied for the majority of my childhood; some of my good childhood friends were white, and I loved the freedom that I experienced when I was with them or their families. Coincidentally, I adopted some of these attributes. I didn't notice this 'adoption' as much when I was younger, but I did respect that our cultures were different, and I appreciated the idea of blending both cultures. In my mind, this was how things were meant to be.

As such, I continued to live and get approval from church friends and family. This caused me a lot of hurt and made me feel insignificant like I didn't belong. I became pretentious but yet hoped that I would be appreciated more, but the opposite happened. People would notice that my character did not match my black friends and, as such, people would find it necessary to point out those difference. Even when my differences were not on display, I still felt separated.

In the previous church, the words spoken by my pastor each week were profound and heard from God many times...

As I stated before, I was a part of the ministry team there, but this was only a title or label that signified my participation. The relationship that I yearned for between the leaders, congregation and myself was not there and I felt as if I was being tolerated for my contributions, but there was no interest in the other ministers in getting to know me on a personal level. I was not worth it in their eyes, or so I was led to believe. Maybe you recall my story about driving in my car after a service, sobbing and praying to God. It was at this time that I asked God, "Why do I feel so empty coming from church?" Well, he heard me and directed me to New Life Christian Church. Not only did He lead me there, but He revealed to me the importance of being myself, living authentically and loving from an authentic place. You see, we were all made in the image of God...whether you are saved (a born again Christian) or not. Which means that our identity is found through Him. The more we learn about the Father, our Abba Father, the more we learn about ourselves and the more we can love from an honest and sincere place. In 2 Corinthians 1:34, it states:

> May the God and Father of our Lord Jesus Christ be Blessed! He is the compassionate Father and God of all comfort. He's the one who comforts us in all our trouble so that we can comfort other people who are

in every kind of trouble. We offer the same comfort that we ourselves received from God.

Instead, we love from a sense of need, which is what I did for the majority of my life.

In the past, I loved out of a need to be accepted and appreciated, but now, I am, learning to love based on the needs I see, which is always a choice; although, it is not an easy one to make. God has taught me that life has less to do with me (which is a selfish human pattern) and more about the majesty of God and the commission He gave to those that love him—to make disciples, ministers to the orphans, and hopeless. This may seem foreign but when you love someone, you don't want them to remain in a state of hurt and despair. God has commissioned us as his children to spread His love of forgiveness so that those who are hurting to can embrace the freedom that can come from uniting with the Father. Love is an act of sacrifice. And He has made the ultimate sacrifice of dying on the cross so that you can be free from your hurt of the past.

That was me. You see—the hopeless! I thought I was good for nothing, and the majority of the time, I felt like I had a disease that repelled people from me. It was the action of people who showed me my worth. Actions spoke louder to me rather than the words people spoke. People and their actions towards me helped me to develop a bad image of myself and guided me in a negative belief about how all people perceived me.

Despite all this, God has taught me how to love well throughout all the emotional and physical pain I have endured during my lifetime. This is not always easy because authentic love directs you to love selflessly; you become more concerned with the person you're directing love towards. I can't say that I always loved in this manner because I was so enthralled with how I was treated by others. It was the understanding of how much God loves and honours me that helped me love from a more genuine place. Godly love that does not compromise who I am in Christ, while still allowing me to impart love on others, not what I think they deserve but a love that stems from who they were created to represent. Genesis 1:27 states, "So God created mankind in His own image, in the image of God he created them; male and female he created them." So today, I love out of the basis that we all were made in God's image and not from the perspective that people have failed or disappointed me.

This was a lesson I learned in my thirties, and I still have to remind myself of this truth today. It was the consistent pain and hurt that I felt, both emotional and physical, that allowed me to acknowledge the rich and faithful love of my—our Abba Father. He can be your father as well.

If you have not received Him yet, Psalms 118:8 (KJV) states, "It is better to trust in the LORD than to put confidence in man," and Psalms 118:6 (KJV) furthers, "The LORD is on my side; I will not fear: what can man do unto me?"

I never thought that it would have been possible to love an unseen God as I do, but the reality is that He has always made me aware of His presence and care. I can honestly say that those walking on Earth (friends and family) have become secondary, and I have begun to see their love as ambiguous and unreliable. I feel like I need to clarify my last statement, although true. It may appear like I have hate and unforgiveness in my heart. I don't. But this freedom that I now experience, a freedom to love wholeheartedly was not always there, and I had to learn the distinction between conditional (human) love and unconditional (Godly) love. As a child, teenager and through parts of my adult life, I was angry, disappointed and frustrated. Growing up, I tended to lean on people and expected them to help me when I needed it and to love me the way I expected to be love. Sounds selfish, doesn't it, and I was. Well, we all can be this way, I guess, can't we? Dictionary.com defines selfishness as being devoted to or caring only for oneself; concerned primarily with one's own interests, benefits, welfare, etc., regardless of others and characterized by or manifesting concern or care only for oneself.

Selfishness is said to be a human tendency, but it was the awareness, realization and grandeurs of God's love that made this hurt disappear. I know this statement might cause some confusion, so let me explain. Selfishness is never a good attribute to have. It is this attribute that inflicts pain on other, without you even realizing it but on the other hand, it is important that you set up healthy boundaries. I heard before that boundaries are like your skin, in that it protects you from toxins in your surrounding from entering into your body. It is therefore possible to love selflessly while still determining what is healthy for your overall holistic wellbeing. To go even further the Bible declares in Mark 12:31, The second is this: 'Love your neighbor as yourself.' There is no commandment greater than these." This is one of the two commands that Jesus gives us in order to have a successful life here on earth. The scripture above also shows that it is not God intention for you to love others and neglect yourself and vice versa. Instead we are instructed to love others the way we expect to receive love. This type of love takes strength, fearlessness and boldness. The Bible says in Isaiah 12:2 (KJV), "Behold, God is my salvation; I will trust, and not be afraid: for the LORD JEHOVAH is my strength and my song; he also has become my salvation."

This became my reality. God saved me, and He continues to introduce to me to the concept of His Genuine Love and what it should look like.

In this process, he is also challenging me to love in the same manner, and so now it is easier to love without having unrealistic expectations for those in my circle (I have to remind myself of the true meaning of love continually). I realize that we have all fallen short from the Glory of God. In other words, as humans, we fail and will continually do so. This is not to undermine the potential of the human race, but it is a tool used to empathize with.

God, the greatest lover, has put it this way in John 13:15 when he said, "Greater love hath no man than this, that a man lay down his life for his friends." This is another verse has been critical for me in understanding love because it shows that love has been extended despite our faults and failures. You see, if Christ could die for us even while we were sinners, while we disappoint Him consistently, then we can love in that manner, too, regardless of how we have been treated, period. I have realized that the way I love and treat others is how I present my love and gratitude towards God the Father.

So, due to the overwhelming love of my Father, I can and constantly love others despite negative treatment, hurt, feelings of abandonment and disappointment. I must caution you that this is not as easy to accomplish as it may sound. It will take awareness and a daily reminder of God's love towards you. The verse 1 John 4:9-11 (English Standard Version) says:

> In this the love of God was made manifest among us, that God sent His only Son into the world, so that we might live through him. In this is love, not that we have loved God but that he loved us and sent His Son to be the propitiation for our sins. Beloved, if God so loved us, we also ought to love one another.

It's a command and expectation that God has placed on us: To love, not selfishly, not so we can receive something in return but because those around us are valuable in the eyes of God. Jesus states that the way you treat your neighbour is the way to treat Him. In Ephesians 5:21, it states, "Submit to one another out of reverence for Christ." The pain I have faced introduced me to the greatest love that we all deserve to experience. "How can that be?" you may be asking. My pain caused me to look up… during disappointment…to look up! It has caused me to rely on a Saviour that has never fail me. At times I felt as if He caressed me into an avenue of hope and deliverance. Even in deplorable situations, He has provided for me, led me and gave me hope. Authentic love and characters of love are shown through God and Christ Jesus. It is through these revelations that I can love more genuinely and authentically. This can be your destiny as well, just look up!

CHAPTER 8

Seeking peace

What is peace? A state of quiet or tranquility, freedom from disturbance or agitation, calm, repose or to make one's peace with, to plead one's cause with, or to become reconciled with another.

These are some definitions given by Webster's Dictionary online. Let look at them closely. These definitions refer to abstaining from distracting noise both in your surroundings and within your mental state.

Growing up, I faced a lot of noise…. Noise (or should I say negativity) from school, from my home, from church, and from so called friends. I felt as if it was all around me like I was a prisoner in solitude within a negative situation and negative thoughts infiltrating my personal space.

In my teenage years, I remember speaking to my best friend (she was someone I would always speak with, and I knew that she was someone I could trust…we were always able to empathize with one another) because she endured similar things. One evening we spoke about the effects that the negativity or the unrelenting discord, the lack of peace, around us. From that time on, we would refer to a song we both adored, entitled "To worship you I live," which spoke about being away from the noise so that we are more able to hear from GOD.

This is the main problem we have today, isn't it? We lack peace in our day-to-day. We are living stressed and worried about tomorrow and how it will look. If you are honest with yourself, you'll admit that life, for the most part, has been unsettling for you. Whether it is living or visiting with people who consistently argue or are negative or you're stressed about your living situation or your job and finances, living this way can alter your peace; it makes you unstable and defers your creativity.

How can you hear from the Creator God when such things are bombarding your mind and heart? Romans 14:19 says, "So then, let us pursue what leads to peace and to mutual edification." Hebrews 12:14 says, "Pursue peace with all men, as well as holiness, without which no one will see the Lord." Psalms 34:14 says, "Turn away from evil and do good. Search for peace, and work to maintain it." These quotes have been a part of my mantra for a while, and it all started in Windsor.

As you might recall, it was in Windsor that my eyes were opened to the love of Christ and the potential that he placed in me. Windsor was a significant time for me because for a while I had no one to lean on but Christ. You could say being in Windsor was one of my loneliest periods in life but quickly became my most fulfilling time because I began leaning on Christ like I never had before. He spoke and directed me when I asked, but it was my state of peace that allowed me to hear him. Being away from chaos gave me the tool(s) I needed to be receptive to His voice and He assisted me to remain in balance. This is not to say that problems didn't arise while I was there, they did, but it wasn't a consistent occurrence. In addition to all this, I created sanctuaries of praise and would talk to God everywhere I went: in my car, on the street walking to school, in my bedroom, talking to friends (most of my friends either came from the Christian group on campus, or we had been to church together). I invited him everywhere because He had become my everything. This is what peace did for me and has been a principle for me ever since.

In returning to Toronto, I wanted to uphold my peace and wanted to make decisions that helped me to maintain it.

One example I have of maintaining peace is a recent testimony that includes my Nissan Versa a.k.a. Bella (that is right, I am one of those people who names their car). After eight months working at a private college through my business, I began looking for a car because I was beginning to fall more often while taking the bus. Relying on my family for rides was inconvenient for both parties involved. I spent months looking for a car and also solicited help from those I went to church with, close friends and family. I determined how much I could spend on a car, what years I wanted, and the types of cars I was interested in. Finally, one presented itself and at the price, I felt comfortable in spending. She was beautiful. A white, compact hatchback, it was so smooth on the road, and I literally got excited test driving it.

But I didn't want to get carried away, so I invited all the males in my family to view this beauty and test drive it with me. This didn't take place in one day; it took roughly 3-4 days for the four males in my life to view this hunk of metal. The day after I signed for the purchase of my car, my supervisor called me into the college for a meeting. I would be lying if I said I wasn't nervous—I was. I guess my nerves came from knowing this position was contract work through my business, and it was less than stable. I sat in the front foyer for five minutes, and then I was called into the office. There, my supervisor told me that, even though she had extended my contact since September (we were now in the month of February), they decided to let me go.

I was devastated. Why did this happen now? How will I pay off for my car now? I had so much to contemplate. As if that wasn't enough, I also had people telling me to cancel the contract with the dealership and others telling to keep it and trust God (which did not help me as much as I thought it would) because I wasn't one who liked to take riskwith my already limited finances. I was always a person that knew what I had and didn't spend over that. So, you see, my predicament was either attaining something I needed or suffering physically but feeling comfortable that my finances were still intact and reassured that I was not going into debt.

This concern subsided after speaking to a friend. His advice to me was to seek peace. He informed me that he didn't feel comfortable telling me how I should make my decision. In fact, his argument was simple: he didn't want to take responsibility for any decision that I made, whether I got the car on the basis of his hypothesis or not. He wanted me to pray and talk to God. To seek His response and to seek His peace over any decision I was about to make. I took this advice and ran with it. I read my Bible, I told God about my frustrations and what I thought I needed, and in the midst of my prayer, I fell asleep. When I woke up, there was a small puddle on my bed where I laid my head…I had been drooling! This was not a normal occurrence for me, so I said to myself in a joking manner, "If this is not peace, I don't know what is." From that time on, I made up my mind that I was keeping my car, and I did. I don't know how I was able to sustain myself until the end of the year, but it happened. I worked casually as a nanny, but that was not sustainable, and my private practice had slowed down, especially after my work at the college, yet the Lord provided for me and more.

Some months after, my mother's friend approached me and asked if I was willing to help her ill father. I told her that I was no longer a practicing PSW or Personal Support Worker, but I would help where I could. They ended up paying me for the work I did. I saw their father almost on a daily basis and for about three to five hours until he passed away. I consider this event a blessing in itself, because of the help I could give her father but also because we got to pray together and discuss Christ and His love. God is so great.

God used a difficult situation of mine and turned it into an opportunity to bless and to refresh this elderly man on his deathbed and also his family. I believe he is in heaven today because of His acknowledgement of Christ on his deathbed. What an opportunity, the opportunity to share God's love with someone that did not have a relationship with Christ. The opportunity to provide him peace and companionship when he was no longer able to take care or sustain himself. This was truly a blessing for me, and I thank God for this opportunity to be His extension of love.

Through this experience, I have realized that life is less about me or you and what we can attain and more about Christ and how he can use us. I believe that it was through my obedience to God during this time that He continued to bless me and after a year God help me to pay off my car in full.

It was a little over a year after I had bought Bella, and it was during income tax season, and I got four checks in the mail, one being my actual tax refund. So, do you remember when I informed you of the period where I was dealing with stomach issues and having the reoccurrence of physical discomfort? Well, the year before paying off my car, I heard disturbing news about my health. In the summer months of 2016, I was going through a series of medical tests. You see, the pain I felt had never ceased; it got to the point where I couldn't stand on my feet in the mornings, where I limped more regularly and used my braces more often. After going through these medical tests, I became aware that I had MSA.

MSA- Muscle System Atrophy is a progressive degenerative neurological disorder that affects multiple areas of the brain. The areas affected are the basal ganglia, cerebellum and brain stem, which are responsible for movement, balance and body functions such as bladder control. Like Parkinson's disease, the automatic nervous system and all that it controls will begin to shut down until death. I have to be very careful here; I don't want to depict any sort of acceptance of this disease.

I say that now, but I must admit that I didn't always have this viewpoint. When I was first told about this by my neurologist, I was devastated and sorrowful. In fact, this news may have had a different effect on me if it was shared with me differently by the specialist. I remember that day like it was yesterday. I went into her office for a followup to the last MRI I did in the hospital (just writing this recaption is causing me to tear). She described the picture that was shown on the MRI as "a hot cross bun." She said that this picture confirmed that I had MSA. "What is that?" I asked. "Exactly what you have described to me, Lorraine," she responded. "So, what can I do to combat this?" I asked. "Nothing," she replied.

I remember leaving her office sad, angry and confused. All I knew was that I had something that was an incurable illness, and it was the reason for the all the pain I had felt my whole life. I went home and did research. I guess my thought was the more I know, the more I could take a hold of this illness and control it. That is not what took place. The more I found out, the more I dug myself into a depression hole, the more silent I became, and the more I wanted to withdraw myself from the ones I loved. If I called someone or if someone called me, I burst out in tears within minutes. Our conversation lasted two to four minutes, tops (and if you knew anything about me, that was not the norm). I must admit of the research I did, I did recognize that some of the activities recommended to those that had this disorder were things I had already begun doing that summer. This alone made me realize that although this news was given to me, God was still a major player in this game call life. It made me realize that God was still looking out for my well-being, by giving me the desire to do certain activities I hadn't attempted in years. This was my glimmer of hope in a very dark place, but at that moment, the darkness was too overwhelming to break free.

The continual need for information concerning this disorder continued for two days straight. The more I found out, the more I cried, "Why is my life ending this way? What about those promises God made to me years ago? I've really felt as if I was on my way to living more holistically." These were some thoughts I had going on that day and the more I thought about these things, the more I felt abandoned and rejected from the One I thought was my sustainer of life. "Why have You forsaken me?" Isn't this what Jesus said when he was on the cross? He was the chosen one, the one who would bring forth peace and redemption to this world but yet had to endure such a shameful and humiliating death.

I pray I am not blaspheming when I say this, but I, too, was holding on to a promise that I know God gave me. But this current predicament looked nothing like a promise; it was shattering, overwhelming, shameful, and discouraging. At that moment, I felt rejection and abandonment from the only one in my life who has shown me unconditional and continuous love. "Has He abandoned me as well?" I thought, "What have I done to deserve all this? I thought I was called for more." I remember going to bed that night with tears and taking countless breaths to reduce the noise that I would have been making, otherwise. I did this so that my family would not be witness to my distress but thank God for rest, and rest is what I experienced that night.

The next morning was a Sunday, and when I arose, there was something noticeably different in my spirit. I don't even recall being sad or the feeling of rejection. I woke up wanting to hear from God, and that is what happened…I read that morning, prayed over myself (declaring God's promises over my life) and then got plugged into listening to Bill Johnson, the senior pastor at a church in northern California. If I remember correctly, the message I heard from him that morning had to do with the weapon of our warfare. I have heard messages about this passage before, especially because I have been in church all my life but this particular morning I remember feeling invincible and awakened through the words spoken. I got ready for church this particular morning with expectation. I knew God would have more to say to me, and I was at a place where I needed to hear more from him.

I'll be honest, I don't remember the message delivered at church that day, but I do remember going up for prayer. That Sunday both of my pastors prayed for me after service as I told them what I heard from the doctor. Before praying for me, they told me that I needed to know that God alone has the final say. They advised me that I shouldn't claim or accept the report from the doctors as mine, and the senior pastor reminded me that I was responsible for what God gave me (my body) and to lose weight, I needed to claim responsibility over what God entrusted me with, and then the rest (the occurrence of healing) I had to leave to God.

Normally, I would be offended by such a comment (due to my own sensitivity and pride), but I knew that he spoke out of love and concern for me. I was about to turn a new leaf in the pages of my life. I was not sure if I was ready to deal with what was up ahead, but I knew I had to go into it with courage and without doubt. As you may know, this is never as easy as one may think it is.

As a result, I knew what I had to do. I chose not to look for work right away and take some time to take care of myself. At the time, I didn't know how long this break would take, but I had to do it. For years, I fought against living a hypocritical life and, therefore, I would take the advice that I once gave my clients in the past. That advice was to take care of your physical needs first before attempting anything else. Although scary, this was now my fate.

At the same time, I also knew I needed to move out of my parents' home. Living with family at thirty-seven years old was causing me more stress (God knows I love them but distance was needed). I found the environment to be toxic at times, and this toxicity was not helping me and my overall health. So, I began speaking to a friend from church about the possibility of rooming with her, and after some time of discussing this with her, she accepted. Another thing that I began looking into was receiving money through the Ontario Disability Support Program (ODSP) because of my decision not to work. This was a hard process to go through, and it shouldn't have been (in my opinion). The first time I heard back from ODSP, they refused me financially. This made me upset. They were essentially saying that my life experiences had no relevance, and I could not accept that either. Can we say confusion? Yep, that was me, confused. On one hand, I didn't want to accept what the doctors were saying, and on the other hand, I wanted acknowledgement for the suffering I had for most of my life. I wrote a letter to ODSP, and basically told them that they should be ashamed of themselves, and on top of that, I would welcome them to witness first hand all that I endure on a daily basis.

Eventually, I was rewarded government assistance and also rewarded money for the months it took for the ODSP to make a decision on my behalf.

It was important for me at the beginning of this particular journey to relay my medical situation only to people of faith. As such, I only told individuals that I knew would pray for my well-being because they themselves were confident in what the Bible said pertaining to health. Jeremiah 33:6 says, "Behold, I bring health and healing, and I will heal them and reveal to them abundance of prosperity and security." I heard it many years ago, and it has always been confirmed to me in the Word of God, that we should always be in agreement with His words! It is important that when we pray that there is an agreement with what He, God, declares in His Word.

In order to see a manifestation of God's word come to life, we must agree with it and this is what I wanted. To have men and women of faith surround me in prayer, men and women who believe what the Word says for our lives and that includes healing. Accordingly, a sister in Christ who knew of my situation informed me of a tax credit that I could be eligible for. Remember my last testimony, the one about me paying off the loan of my car? Well, this is how it all began. I didn't have to have a formal diagnosis for this credit at this time (it was a few months before I heard the doctor's report). What I needed was to declare that I had health issues in the past, and I could be rewarded a huge lump sum of money for the years indicated. As I applied for this credit, it came to my attention by the intake that because I was not working a nine to five job for several years that I would get little to no money at all. In the end, they estimated that I would get nearly a thousand dollars from this tax credit. Time went by, and I never heard back from this particular agency until the following year.

For me, this is just another example of God's wondrous grace in my life and in the lives of those in his family. I feel as if God knew, in retrospect, about all the medical endurances that I would have to go through. As such, he was faithful to me, just as he has been in my previous years. Now let's return to my testimony of paying off my car in full a year after I financed it (without any substantial income).

Two weeks or so after filing for my income tax, I received twice the amount in my bank than what I was told by my accountant.

I found this strange but also realized that Revenue Canada could have recalculated my forms and determined that I was getting more. This was a blessing in itself, and I didn't question it any further. A week after the first deposit, I noted that I got another deposit from Revenue Canada. This time it was the exact amount that I was quoted by my accountant. Okay, now I am suspicious was the thought that went through my head. I didn't waste any time. I called Revenue Canada because the worst thing that can ever happen to someone would be to have to pay back Revenue Canada.

"Hi," I said as the person on the receiving end of my call. "I have noticed that within the past three weeks, I have received two deposits from Revenue Canada. Has there been some mistake? Do I owe you money?"

"No," the gentleman responded. "Have you applied for the disability tax credit?"

"Yes," I responded with confusion.

"Well, this is where the extra money came from,"

"OKAY!! Thank you." I was stunned because I received more than double the amount I was quoted the previous summer by the intake team. Despite this surprise, I thanked God and paid off some bills in full. Aside from my car's monthly payment and my school fees, I was free from debt. I was so grateful and thanked God for working such a miracle, but the story does not end there. Obviously, because I was still paying for a car note. About a month later, I get a call from the company that originally helped me fill out the application. This happened on a Friday after Bible study at church. The caller asserted that I would receive more money from Revenue Canada. I asked her if this was correct because I have already received money from them. She insisted that I was to receive another lump sum of money, but she was not able to give me the exact amount. In delusional excitement, I returned back to the company of my brothers and sisters in Christ. In a week or less, I received over $18,000 in my bank account. Roughly, that was a total of $22,000 that I received from the government in a month. There you have it, the wonders of God's love. He is always working things out for those that love the Lord and are called according to His purpose (Romans 8:28). I have many more examples of stepping into faith for peace and God met me there. I would not change a thing about my past because it has awakened me to the inconceivable, passionate Love of the Father towards those that trust in him.

CHAPTER 9

The fear of the Lord (what it really means)

I grew up in a church that taught that God was condemning and judgmental. I went to church regularly with my family, and we also had Sunday morning prayer regularly at home before leaving the house for church. Church was our lifestyle. And yet there was so much fear that I endured regularly, fear that I was not living up to my role as a pastor kid, fear that I wasn't good enough to be accepted by my peers, fear I was a burden to other people, fear that I was not living up to God's standards, fear I would not succeed in my academics, fear that no one would love me for who I was, just so many fears.

These fears caused me to shy away from public speaking, having and maintaining close male relationships, even though I was the only girl child in my family and grew up with many guys surrounding me in church. In addition to the above, I feared rejection, and this, I believe, was my greatest fear of all.

Remember my famous phrase in high school, "I just wanna love to be loved." Well, that was me in a nutshell. I had a desire to love people, but I also wanted to receive that back, but I became awkward and fragile when love was not shown back to me. I was a super-sensitive child and, as such, my emotions were finicky and fickle.

Eventually, what I saw as reality became contingent on how I felt, and they guided my thought process, whether healthy or unhealthy, and trust me, my thoughts where mainly unhealthy. It's hard to believe that the fear of one thing can lead to so many subfears, which lead to my being a perfectionist. Perfectionist? Are you scratching your head yet? Let me help. Perfectionism is not being perfect all the time. Rather, it is a standard of high regard that a person sets for himself or herself. This may look like a good thing but, in actuality, perfectionism can assist you in undermining yourself and can hinder your risk taking abilities.

Aside from the certainty I had when entering university (God confirmed to me His guidance, presence and protection in this particular opportunity), I was uncertain in almost everything I attempted and usually proclaimed that the end result would be a negative one, and it usually was. Years of hearing, living and embracing negative words and thoughts began to overwhelm me, and my inner peace was not a standard. As such, peace was something I fought to obtain and experience.

The Bible states that "perfect love casts out all fears" (1 John 4:18 ESV). What? I have been alive for thirty-nine years now. Where's my violin? And I have not experienced a love that would overcome my fears. I am grateful that God has kept me for thirty-nine years, but I have not found a love that was perfect, not until I cultivated a relationship with my Abba Father, Daddy

God: My God. I am not really sure how this transition happened, but the fear I had of God's wrath when I was younger dissipated.

I believe God took time out to reintroduce me to His grace and love. He allowed me to see the constant inconsistencies and sometimes neglect from humans in my surroundings and as much as I hate to admit this, this is the painful truth. He also replaced them with His favour and love. I came to the realization through His grace that He, Abba who is majestic and Holy, honoured me. That thought blew me away. Why? Why would someone who has the highest standard, someone who is highly regarded and omnipresent, look down on me and honour me? Love, His love is the greatest love you can ever imagine. I have to be honest with you, I have always wanted to love and be loved, but now being thirty-nine years young and single, I love because I am loved by God. This journey has been a hard one, and I would probably need to write another book in order to explain my process to you, but it was this unconditional, consistent, tangible love that has caused me to surrender to a God that cannot be seen.

He has introduced Himself to me and has embraced me for who I am, I didn't have to pretend, hide or assume another personality. He loved me without me being perfect, whether I was rich or poor, able or disabled. He saw me for me! For the first time, I realized someone saw me and loved me for me. It wasn't pity or sympathy either; it was the purest and rich action of love. So how does one respond to this expression of love? You respond by loving back as best as you can; you become mesmerized and in awe of the person (God is a person). You alter your decisions and make choices because of His encompassing love and His unalterable words. Slowly, you'll notice that the things that drowned you in fears are being liberated, and you'll notice that you are now are at peace within yourself. Believe it or not, the above describes the fear of the Lord.

Proverbs 8 (NKJV) summarizes well what the fear of the Lord means for both you and me. It is no wonder why the Bible states in 1 John 4:18 and 2 Corinthians 3:17 that "perfect Love casts out all fears" or where the spirit of the Lord is there is freedom. Embracing God's truth liberates us from fear and mental torments! But this does not come easily. Reminding yourself of God's love, allowing His words to marinate in your soul, and resting in the peace he has provided for us allows us to remain in this undeniable joy and trust.

The other day, after doing a fast and prayer with my church, I was tormented with anxiety and evil thoughts. My past was haunting me after I would experience an uplifting time with the Lord. During my fasting, I believe that God was reiterating to me things that we need to be doing as a church, a functioning body, which obviously includes you and me. Well, during our prayer week, I prayed out in the open. This was a bold move for me. Remember how I stated earlier that I was afraid of public speaking? Why would I want to put myself through such torment? Well, I was beginning a new stage. I wanted to do what the Holy Spirit was influencing me to do, and that night I was inspired to pray, amidst my fears, I did it. Funny enough, I heard a sermon that spoke on taking risks and the preacher exclaimed that without risk there can be no growth. Let's make no mistake: I wanted to grow, and so I took the risk, but it came with a lot of doubts and torments. Before I left the church, I felt as if people were forming judgments about me, talking about me and slandering me. These were my own thoughts after that prayer. I guess I wanted recognition for the prayer that I did and when I did not get that, thoughts of insecurity flooded my mind. I got into my car and began to share my feelings with God.

I asked God to take out anything in me that was not of Him. I spoke to him about my newfound desire to do His will, at all costs but did not want these thoughts of mine to discourage my efforts. While talking to God, I went blank and stared out into the streets as I drove. Why were these thoughts invading my mind and causing anxiousness in me? Being analytical, I doubted my own motives for praying at church. Was it God motivating me? By the time I got home, I had a really bad headache. I thought, maybe, I was hungry since I had eaten dinner at 3 p.m. and now it was well after 9 p.m. So, I ate some nuts and drank some water, but the headache was still prominent. With my headache still pounding (I assume a product of my anxiety), I decided that I needed to rest in His, God's, presence, so I listened to worship songs and read scripture that would console my troubled mind, which they did. Towards the end of the night, I got on my hand and knees, lay on my belly as I listened to a message entitled "Fear of God vs the fear of man." A message I found as I was streaming online. Again, I am not sure when this took place, but there was a calmness in my mind, and without even finishing listening to the preacher, I headed off to bed and had a good night's sleep. My point is that fears will come; they happen, but they don't have to become a lifestyle. This statement becomes a reality when you become aware of the awe-inspiring love of God.

In the small group that I lead, I like to phrase it in this way: The love of God can be compared to finding a lover in that when He pours out His love for you and me, our automatic response is to love and honour that person in return because of the constant love provided to us. This is the true depiction of the Fear of the

Lord…Honour. According to the New American Standard Old Testament Hebrew Lexicon, one definition of fear is to stand in awe of, be in awe or to reverence, to fear, to honour. In the Greek, Phobos equals fear. And it can be described in two ways: 1. Fear, dread, terror 2. that which strikes terror or reverence for one's partner.

The Bible repeatedly connotes reverence for God. For example, Luke 7:36-50 is a good example of this, telling the story of a known "sinful woman" who honoured God with all that she had, a perfumed ointment which she used before he was to die on the cross. This act was a sign of reverence, awe and fear of the Lord. For her, this was a sign of surrendering all she had before the living King.

Intrinsically, honour should influence you to surrender, follow His words, to apply them to your daily life and to humble yourself before Him. He, Christ, becomes your status quo, and there becomes a desire to follow His lead. As such, Christ comforts and provides peace continually. It is His truth and His Word that will set you free, literally. Psalms 33:9 says, "Let all the earth fear the Lord, let all the inhabitants of the world stand in awe of him." Proverbs 1:7 states, "The fear of the Lord is the beginning of knowledge, fools despise wisdom and instruction." These are words to live by, and as you do, you will notice that there is an experience of liberty from worldly fears, in other words, fear of man. A renewed peace and trust in the Lord and His promises will enable you to "fear the Lord."

I hope that you are getting this. The fear of the Lord that is spoken about in the Word of God is actually honour and trust in who He is. Honour and trust produce love, peace and wholeness.

Biblical fear is the total opposite of what the world describes as fear and negates anxiety, worry, depression and the like.

I am not a biblical scholar, but my many experiences have brought me to this understanding. And accordingly, I thank God for all of my heartaches in life because it has brought me to an understanding of My True Lover, My God and Friend. I would not trade that experience for anything. Psalms 63:3 declares, "Because your love is better than life, my lips will praise you." Isn't that amazing? To experience a love that is so outrageous that it begins to change and rectify the hurt and hatred that once flooded your mind and heart. A love that demands wholeness and restoration. In my opinion, there is no human love that can compare to this.

Regardless of the pages and testimonies of God's provision in this book, my life cannot be described as perfect. In fact, I believe that the more I see God blessing my life, the more the devil tries to discourage me. But the scripture in 1 John 4:4 has become my anthem, says, "Little children, you are from God and have overcome them, for he who is in you is greater than he who is in the world."

Conclusion

Honesty has always been my important to me. Accordingly, I try to be forthright in everything I do. With that said, I will tell you that during last stages the of writing this book I was still on government funding and was not working. Living on my own but dependent on the government for my livelihood. In actuality, my business has ceased to exist, and I closed my online presence due to a lack of financial stability. But once this book was finished and after I began looking for a publisher, I prayed that God would assist me financially, especially because I desired to promote God's goodness through this book in an effective way. After this prayer, and two weeks later, I received an email from Newtopia, a wellness company that promotes holistic living to companies across the US. I applied for this job two years prior to this email, so after two years and two weeks, I started working there as an inspirator assisting people to lose weight and live a healthier lifestyle. Isn't God awesome?

Although far from perfect, my family and I see each other on a weekly basis (sometimes more). Almost every Sunday, although we go to different churches; we get together for our family dinners enjoying each other's company. My mom and I speak to each other practically every day and my dad calls or sends texts to encourage me on my journey or share uplifting words with me. I am truly blessed and see miracles around me every day, and I know God is not finished yet, with me or my family. The Bible says in Psalms 37:1-6:

> Trust in the LORD and do good; dwell in the land and cultivate faithfulness. Delight yourself in the LORD, and He will give you the desires of your heart. Commit your way to the LORD; trust in Him, and He will do it. He will bring forth your righteousness like the dawn, your justice like the noonday sun.

This means he will renew or redeem your life from suffering or past predicaments and place you where you need to be.

My life has not been very easy…and I am not comparing my life to another; this would be an unfair thing to do because I do understand that God gives us different measures of faith. Roman 12:3 says, "Because of the privilege and authority God has given me, I give each of you this warning: Don't think you are better than you really are. Be honest in your evaluation of yourselves, measuring yourselves by the faith God has given us."

But my hope in writing this book was to encourage you not to give up on hope and ultimately, never to give up on God. Without a true knowledge of God and His love for us, it is easy to go through life working to attain "stuff," living a life that is full of stress and agony and remaining in a hopeless state.

It is important to realize that this was never God's intention for you or me. In fact, let's dismiss the ideology that God bring disaster and destruction. If this is something you have thought about, please ask God to reveal to you His true nature. Truth be told, you and I were created for the sole purpose of having a relationship with God. And as such, He has determined a way for you and me to be drawn back to Him, despite our sinful nature. Jesus is that way. Jesus Christ came to not only take our place but also to die for our sins. The statement "Jesus Christ came to take our place" means that He came to stand in our stead. Jesus is the only perfect being, the One who did no wrong and committed no sin. Knowing this now, you can imagine that when God looks upon us, what He sees is Jesus Christ and not the sins we have committed. This is great news! Because we do not have to work hard to be in right standing with God. We need to trust in His finish work.

After getting saved at seventeen years old, I had always wondered what Christ meant when he said, "It is finished" on the cross. It was a statement that baffled my mind for years…And when I asked some of my elders growing up…I was never satisfied with the answer given, the answer never satisfied my spirit/my soul. If I am honest, although it been difficult for me, it was my journey (as well as for the people I met along the way) that helped me come to the amazing conclusion that Christ did all the necessary work for me. I simply have to trust and be obedient to Him and His Word.

Secretly, you know what I love to see? I love to see peoples' expressions when I tell them that I had a huge temper, and I was a bully. They look at me as if to say, "I thought you were a Christian…why are you lying to me right now?" Sometimes it's hard for me to believe in the anger I harboured for so many years, but it was true. Now, when you see me the opposite is true. I do get angry sometimes; yes, but it cannot be compared to my early teenage years. My parents did not enroll me in a program, nor did I see a counsellor for any of my negative outbursts. I simply surrendered to God.

The art of surrender is a process, and I am sure someone can write a book on it. Nevertheless, it is not an eleven steps stage, it can be categorized as an enlightening or illumination of God and who He is. This illumination occurs at different periods in our lives. Earlier in this book, I described God as love. It is my belief that once you become aware of His Continual Love, surrendering becomes second nature to us. This has been my reality and something that I whole-heartedly believe in.

If you're a woman, I am sure you can relate to what I am about to say. As a young girl, I always dreamed of a knight in shining amour who would come and rescue me…am I the only one? Well, Jesus has become that to me…this may sound far-fetched, but it was the constant rejection I felt and saw growing up that redirecting my eye to Christ. And His love is not something I read, but it became a tangible reality …I have felt Him…over and over again. He has rescued me and continues to do so, although I live in a world that seems self absorbed and compassionless.

I am a person who loves to share good news; in fact, some would say that I get excited easily, and it's true! If I go shopping, and I see a sale, I want to inform people around me of that sale because life can be tough, financially. In the same way, I have to share the love of Christ…. He rescued me from a life of hurt and disappointment. Sadly, our world is filled with hurt, tormented, and mentally ill people who need to be rescued, and Christ is the answer to those burdens. You don't have to remain trapped in a box, as I once was, wanting to be freed but could not. You don't have to be tormented with fears that restrict you from taking a step because you were not sure what the outcome would be; you don't have to live under the opinion of others who dictate what your next step should be. You can be freed, as I was freed, though the Love of a Saviour who has not bound you but has set you free. Free to live as He has called you to live, free to be who He has designed you to be, free to love as He has loved, free from past hurt and ridicule, and above all, free from sin and a lifetime of torment.

Can I introduce you to a friend who sticks closer to you than a brother? His Name is Christ Jesus…Emanuel, the Saviour of this world. God sent Jesus to Earth as a way to bring us back to God, to have fellowship with God, and as such, he promises to keep us in perfect peace. In John 8:19, Jesus states, "…Since you don't know who I am, you don't know who my Father is. If you knew me, you would also know my Father." This verse reminds us that as you get to know Jesus, He will introduce you to God the Father. Jesus stands as the only gateway to Our Abba Father… and he is waiting for you!

What do you have to lose? Your pride, your shame, your insecurities…aren't they worth doing away with? You can accept Christ into your heart today…Say, "Lord, I need you and desire my life to be different! I am a sinner, and I want to feel your great embrace. I believe that you died to save us from this world, and I want to be a part of your great family…Amen!" If you read that with honest conviction…

Congratulations, you are saved! Yes, it's that easy. Find a good Bible teaching church, a church that desires to disciple you and help you grow in faith. The Bible says that angels rejoice for those who come to the knowledge of Our Saviour, and I am rejoicing with you, today! Welcome to the family of God, and I pray that God will surround you and bless you abundantly on this unpredictable but peacefilled journey called life.

Be blessed.

www.ingramcontent.com/pod-product-compliance
Lightning Source LLC
LaVergne TN
LVHW011728060526
838200LV00051B/3070